The Mind and Method of the Legal Academic

The Mind and Method of the Legal Academic

Jan M. Smits

Maastricht University, The Netherlands

Edward Elgar

Cheltenham, UK • Northampton, MA, USA

Published by
Edward Elgar Publishing Limited
The Lypiatts
15 Lansdown Road
Cheltenham
Glos GL50 2JA
UK

Edward Elgar Publishing, Inc.
William Pratt House
9 Dewey Court
Northampton
Massachusetts 01060
USA

A catalogue record for this book
is available from the British Library

Library of Congress Control Number: 2012938066

FSC
www.fsc.org
MIX
Paper from
responsible sources
FSC® C018575

ISBN 978 0 85793 654 7 (cased)

Typeset by Servis Filmsetting Ltd, Stockport, Cheshire
Printed and bound by MPG Books Group, UK

Contents

Preface

This book deals with the aims, methods and organization of legal scholarship. This theme has received a lot of attention in the last few years but the primary goal of this work is not to offer an elaborate overview of these recent discussions, which have taken place in various countries. Instead, the following pages offer a – sometimes personally inspired – essay on the diverse aspects of doing academic work in the field of law. The core of the argument is that legal science should primarily deal with the 'ought' question: 'What is it that people and organizations are legally obliged to do?' This question cannot be answered by mere reference to national legislation or case law, but should always be based on arguments derived from other sources. This makes the legal discipline a highly international one: it does not deal with the positive law of one or more jurisdictions, but with what is law in general. The many conclusions that follow from this abstract summary will be discussed in much detail in this book. It deals with questions such as, 'What is the core of the legal approach?' and, 'To what extent does the law meet the requirements of an academic discipline?' and addresses the organization and assessment of legal research and the importance of debate.

It was a pleasure to write this book. Having worked in various law schools in the past twenty years, I felt the need to proffer my own views of legal scholarship. This led to insights that were sometimes surprising even to myself. I hope that readers will find in this book some of the inspiration that I experienced while writing it although, to be frank, some may say that I conceded too much to Herman Melville's well-known aphorism that it is better to fail in originality than to succeed in imitation.

I was able to test the thoughts laid down in this book at meetings in Helsinki (KATTI, 21 March 2007), Montréal (McGill Round Table on Legal Education, 27–28 September 2007), Maastricht (Conference Methods of Human Rights Research, 24 November 2007), Florence (EUI, 26 November 2007), Stellenbosch (STIAS, 6–8 December 2007), Tilburg (Research Group on Methodology of Law and Legal Research, 4 March 2008), Utrecht (SIM, 8 April 2008), Rovaniemi (conference on 30 years of legal education in the University of Lapland, 16 March 2009), Lammi (Nordic Graduate School, 19–20 March 2009) and London (Centre for Transnational Legal Studies, 20 April 2011). An amended Dutch version of this book (published as *Omstreden Rechtswetenschap*) was presented at Tilburg University on 25 November 2009 by way of comments made by Monica Claes, Jan Vranken, Eric van Damme and Edgar Du Perron. I profited a great deal from these meetings, as I did from the comments made by Christa Dubois, Jaap Hage, Jaakko Husa, Milan Janco, Mark Kawakami, Eric Tjong Tjin Tai and Jan Vranken. Mark Kawakami also provided excellent language editing.

Maastricht, May 2012

Introduction: a discipline in crisis?

1. An Identity Crisis

Traditional legal scholarship is under pressure. In several countries around the world, a debate has evolved about the aims and methods of the academic study of law. There are various aspects to this debate. One question is, what should legal academics be concerned with: the traditional study of legislation and case law and its accommodation in the legal 'system' (an activity that is increasingly regarded as lacking in creativity), or with much more elevated themes? Another question is about the methods that should be used in legal research and how this research should be assessed, prompting the question, which research is 'better' and why should this be the case? There have also been pleas to organize the legal discipline more in line with other fields, including the introduction of rigorous peer review and the classification of journals. Finally, some have made the claim that legal academics should also be substantively more oriented towards other fields (in particular the social sciences) and that legal scholarship should develop as an international discipline instead of one primarily dealing with only one national law.

This debate is taking place in several European countries and, in particular, in the United Kingdom and the Netherlands. According to Becher (1989, 30), legal academics are seen by their other colleagues in the university as 'not really academic. (. . .) Their scholarly activities are thought to be unexciting and uncreative, comprising a series of intellectual puzzles scattered along "large areas of description"'. Twining (1994, 141) characterizes the traditional academic approach to law as 'narrow, conservative, illiberal, unrealistic and boring', with too much attention being given to technical details and too little to the 'big' questions. In the Netherlands, the discussion is at least partly the result of the financial consequences attached to the uncertain status of the legal discipline: lawyers often have difficulty in convincing representatives of other disciplines, university administrators and funding organizations of the quality of their work. See, for a similar debate in Germany: Ipsen (2005), Engel & Schön (2007), and Bernhart (2008); and for a general perspective on methodology, Van Hoecke (2011). In France, a related discussion is taking place about the merits of doctrinal work: see Jestaz & Jamin (2004); Pimont (2006); and Muir-Watt (2011). Van Gestel and Micklitz (2011) make the claim that doctrinal legal research should be revitalized.

The debate about the aims and methods of legal scholarship is not limited to Europe. While, in several European countries, the academic study of law is often seen as not academic enough, the usual criticism in American law schools is that there is too much attention to theory and interdisciplinarity in teaching and research.

The starting point for this debate in the United States is arguably the well-known article written by Judge Harry T. Edwards (1992), in which he fulminates about the gap between legal practice and the, in his view, often irrelevant and mediocre interdisciplinary work published in the more prestigious law reviews. In addition, he argued that future lawyers will no longer receive an adequate legal education that prepares them to practice law as the national law schools have been moving towards educating academics instead of lawyers. According to Edwards (1992, 56), however, '"personal fascination" is not a justification for scholarship, of any kind'. Deborah Rhode (2002, 1340) also complains that too much legal research is not done well: 'it exhaustively exhumes unimportant topics or replicates familiar arguments on important ones'.

Although the debate about aims and methods of academic work in law has received new impetus in the last decade, it is not a new discussion. At least since the beginning of the nineteenth century, the tocsin has sounded over the status of the legal discipline. Well-known are the cries of distress by Von Kirchmann ('The Worthlessness of Jurisprudence as a Body of Knowledge') in 1848 and by Lundstedt ('The Non-Academic Character of the Legal Discipline') in 1932. In the Netherlands, it was Taco Mulder who, in 1937, published a brochure with the title 'I Accuse the Faculty of Law of Being Non-Academic'. While the arguments of these authors are diverse, they all enter into combat with traditional legal scholarship.

> The plea of Von Kirchmann in 1848 best fits the present discussion: its main point is that legal science differs from most other academic disciplines because it is the 'maid of the coincidence' as it primarily deals with solving uncertainties and gaps in the positive law. This makes jurists – in Von Kirchmann's figurative language – like worms that live only from the putrid wood in the positive law, in his view a situation fatal to the academic character of jurisprudence. In his famous words: 'As the science makes the coincidental its article, it becomes coincidental itself; three words changed by the law-maker, and whole libraries become rubbish' (p. 24).
>
> Lundstedt's criticism on the other hand is inspired by a specific (empirical) view of science: because legal academics deal with justice, and justice is not an observable phenomenon, it is not real science. The only thing possible is then a 'positive science of law' (Adolf Merkel). Others (including those adhering to Austin's analytical legal philosophy), however, have fundamentally disputed this view of what makes a field academic.

It is important to make clear what this criticized 'traditional' legal science is really about. The criticism is usually directed to the doctrinal approach, in which rules, principles and case law are considered from the *internal* perspective and in which law is looked at as being in a relatively autonomous relation to the social, economic and political reality. It is the positive law as given by legislatures and courts that forms the starting point for any meaningful analysis. This positive law can of course be criticized, but legal academia accepts the bulk of it as *given* and legal practice itself can profit from doctrinal criticism and systematization. The search for coherence in the given materials is thus seen as an important, if not the most important, part of academic work.

McCrudden (2006, 633) recently described traditional legal science as a discipline of 'critical reasoning based around authoritative texts'. Two aspects are important to emphasize. The first is the central role of legislature and the courts: their decisions can be criticized, but in the end their texts do have authority. Cf. Posner (1990, 83): 'To be blunt, the ultimate ratio of law is indeed force' and the classic statement by Hobbes in *A Dialogue Between a Philosopher and a Student of the Common Laws of England* (1681, [2005, 55]): 'It is not wisdom, but authority that makes a law.' The second aspect is that this doctrinal approach has its own methodology. Even though it may not be clear what this legal methodology exactly consists of (it entails a certain way of interpretation, systematization and argumentation), there is little doubt that it is an *autonomous* methodology: reference to other than the own, legal, sources is not needed. Cf. Posner (2002, 1316) and Ibbetson (2003, 864), and for the internal perspective also *infra*, no. 10.

2. Legal Science at the Crossroads

The arguments made above substantiate the conclusion that the legal discipline suffers from an identity crisis: not only do outsiders accuse legal science of being unacademic, but also legal scholars themselves no longer seem to know which discipline they practice. This crisis is surprising. A midlife crisis it cannot be: the academic study of law has existed since the very founding of the University in the Middle Ages. What is more, empirical science itself originally derived its methods from the law, through scholars like Francis Bacon. In the nineteenth century, legal science was seen as one of the most important achievements of human civilization and even superior to many other academic disciplines.

> This was not only true for continental Europe but also in the Anglo-American world. David Dudley Field (1859, 13–14) thus stated about legal scholarship: 'Compare this science with any of the other sciences; with those which are esteemed the greatest in extent, and the most exalted in subject. Take even astronomy, that noble science (. . .). Sublime as this science is, it is but the science on inanimate matter, and a few natural laws; while the science which is the subject of our discourse governs the actions of human beings, intelligent and immortal, penetrates into the secrets of their souls, subdues their wills, and adapts itself to the endless variety of their wants, motives and conditions'.

The image that the outside world has of legal academics is apparently no longer based on these (or other) merits. The general tendency is to say that 'real' knowledge cannot be based upon conceptual constructions, the finding of coherence, or the development of abstract theories (all important parts of the 'internal' approach to law) but should rest on empirical work instead. This was well expressed by the famous theoretical physicist, Richard Feynman, when he deemed experiment to be 'the sole judge of scientific truth'. Although this debate about the nature of academic work has been in existence since the seventeenth century, it seems that law is now much more influenced by empiricism than it was in the past.

One result of this influence is that we now also see a shift from traditional legal scholarship towards a more interdisciplinary and empirical approach. It seems that legal science is at a crossroads in its long career. As Thomas Ulen states: 'Legal scholarship is on the verge of a dramatically different manner of doing routine legal investigation. Put in a nutshell, that change is to make law much like the other disciplines in the university that believe themselves to be practicing "science" (. . .)' What Ulen describes has already largely materialized in the United States and is seen by many as an attractive way forward for Europe as well.

> See Feynman (1964) and Ulen (2002, 2); cf. Stolker (2003) for the Netherlands and Cownie (2004, 72) for the United Kingdom.

This begs the question to what extent the traditional, doctrinal, method of doing academic work in law can survive if other methods of research can claim more recognition from the academic community. Empirical and interdisciplinary work in law (including 'law and . . .' approaches) already has a clearly higher status in the United States than doctrinal work. The *locus classicus* for a survey of this development is Posner (1987). This also means that law is increasingly becoming the domain of economists, philosophers, sociologists and psychologists. McCrudden (2006, 641) sees this development even as '(. . .) the growth of an approach to law that may challenge the idea of legal scholarship as a separate craft'. See also, for a possible explanation of this development, Lawrence Lessig (2011).

3. A Rediscovery of the Legal Approach?

The previous sections provide the background for this book. The main question addressed in the following section is whether traditional legal science is an autonomous discipline and, if so, to what extent. Moreover, the question is asked, what are the aims and methods of traditional work in law and how do they relate to other academic approaches to law and to other fields (such as economics and empirical sciences)? The answer requires an extensive discussion of various aspects of present academic practice as well as a more personal vision of what legal research should be about. This means that the argument put forward in this book is rather personal.

This book is difficult to categorize. It deals with aspects of legal theory, legal methodology and the sociology of science, but also with positive law and policy questions. Examples come mainly (but not exclusively) from the field of private law.

The main thesis of this book is that the development sketched above, in which external approaches towards law get the upper hand, is a dangerous one. There is little doubt that the law can profit from the insights of other disciplines. However, this does not mean that the normative approach towards law should be abandoned. On the contrary: the core question should not be how *other* disciplines can help us in making the academic study of law more 'scientific' but how the legal approach itself can better meet the expectations that one may have of an academic discipline. Put in a somewhat paradoxical manner: there is every reason to rediscover the *legal* approach to the law.

The idea that legal academics should primarily look at other disciplines for a recalibration of their field is widespread. Richard Posner is closely associated with this view. Cf. *infra*, no. 25.

4. Structure of the Argument

Before discussing my own view of what legal science is about, it is useful to describe the various types of legal scholarship that are feasible. Chapter I describes these types of research by looking at their aims and methodology. Chapter II is devoted to what is, in my view, the main aim of legal scholarship: to reflect upon the normative question of what the law *ought* to be. Chapter III builds upon this view by going into the accompanying methodology. To conclude, Chapter IV is devoted to a discussion of the main consequences of this view for the organization of legal research and teaching, and for the value of creative research and methodology. The synopsis revisits the claim that legal science is in a state of crisis: the arguments presented throughout the book will allow us to exhibit a definitive answer to the question and to the extent of the predicament.

I. Legal science: a typology

1. INTRODUCTION

5. Four Types of Legal Scholarship

It is clear that the term 'legal scholarship' covers many different types of research. And yet, there is only paltry discussion about how to categorize the various research efforts in law. This chapter aims to distinguish between ways of doing legal research on the basis of the questions one can ask about the law.

The classification of legal research can also be based on other criteria. A common one is to follow the ever-increasing subdivisions within the legal field. In so far as the existence of separate professorial chairs and law journals is a criterion for qualifying a field as a separate sub-discipline, one can only conclude that many new fields have emerged in the last fifty years. Everything that, until the 1950s, was often covered by only one chair on private law now tends to be cut up into separate fields of contract law, tort law, property law, land law, family law, company law (often again split up into corporate governance, transport law, insurance law, intellectual property law, and so on), and insolvency law. An alternative to this is the so-called functional fields approach, where the laws are categorized according to some societal issue, as in the case of social law, construction law and environmental law, or in line with a certain category of people, as in consumer law, juvenile law, migration law and the field of law and feminism. These categorizations have little relevance to questions about the aim and method of legal research for they only deal with the substantive matter of what is being investigated, and not with the investigation itself.

Four questions can be asked about law.

1. How does the law read? The aim of this type of scholarship is to *describe*. This does not necessarily have to be the law of one's own jurisdiction as it stands today: it is also possible to describe the contract law of the province of Holland in the seventeenth century or the present-day criminal law of Singapore. A large part of traditional legal science deals with the description of the positive law.
2. How ought the law to read? Next to describing the law, legal academics deal with the normative question of how the law *should* read. It is quite common to find in an article or a book both descriptions and judgements, together, about how the law ought to read. A commentary on a judicial opinion will usually not only describe it in the light of the 'system' of law, but it will also criticize it and indicate how things could be done differently. I will claim that the normative question is at the core of legal science but that, in answering the question, legal academics over-emphasize the role of present-day law in their analysis (see *infra*, Chapter II).
3. What are the consequences of applying a certain legal rule? This question leads on to the effect of law on society. This, so-called, empirical legal science is becoming increasingly popular among academics.
4. What is law? When is it valid and how does it develop? These questions are about the (political and moral) legitimacy of law, its relationship with other normative systems (such as morality) and the influence of factors like history, society and economy on the development of law. This type of scholarship usually tries to *explain* the law from an external perspective. Philosophy of law and legal theory are the fields that traditionally deal with this.

It should be noted that philosophy of law can be both descriptive and normative. Rubin (1996, 571) shows that H.L.A. Hart's *The Concept of Law* (1997) of 1961, which was written as a textbook for first year students, only pretends to describe the existing law, while Finnis' *Natural Law and Natural Rights* (1980) clearly shows how the existing legal system should be changed.

I emphasize that this classification of legal questions into different types of 'research agendas' is not the sole conceivable method. A common distinction is the one that is made between research into the positive law and into interdisciplinary and multidisciplinary research. While the first is directed to the study of the present law, interdisciplinary research crosses the boundaries between the law and other disciplines (as legal history and legal anthropology have done for a long time and as the newly established fields of Law and Economics, and Law and Psychology also aim to do). The less ambitious multidisciplinary research does not aim to investigate a topic in a truly integrated manner but merely looks at a question from different angles. These approaches are in my view mere methods of research that can be brought into action for all types of research agenda. Thus, a description of the positive law can take place by making use of a 'black letter' approach, but can also be done in a multidisciplinary way (see *infra*, no. 11 ff.). In the same way, the normative question about the 'ought' can be answered both by looking at the positive law (What ought to be, according to the law in force?) and in a more fundamental way (What ought the law to be like if we leave the positive law aside?).

Rubin (1996, 562; cf. McCrudden 2006) makes use of a similar classification. In the social sciences it is more common to make classifications of types of research questions. They usually distinguish between four types of research (Ruane, 2005, 12 ff.):

- *exploration*: the discovery of new data. This usually leads to so-called qualitative information: data that can be described in words;
- *description*: description of a phenomenon or of an experiment. In social science this is often (though not exclusively) put in quantitative terms;
- *explanation*: the search for explanations of what has been described;

- *evaluation*: the search for the practical results that the research can have.

> This classification has only limited value for legal scholarship. This is because research in law is usually not directed to a description or explanation of *facts*, but rather aims to dispute *ideas* (see *infra*, Chapter III). A fine overview of the enormous diversity of legal research is offered by Siems (2008), on which *infra*, no. 51.

The next three sections deal with three of the research agendas identified above. In each section, we will also ask which methods can be used to follow these agendas. Because of the great importance of the second question (the normative question of how the law ought to read), this one will be discussed separately in Chapter II.

2. DESCRIPTIVE LEGAL SCIENCE

6. Introduction

This section is devoted to so-called descriptive legal science, usually seen as a synonym for a legal doctrinal approach or for legal systematization: the systematic description of the law in a certain field. This type of legal scholarship is often no longer regarded as particularly prestigious. And yet, it is the type of work that most closely resembles the perception of scientific method in other disciplines *and* that is still practiced most commonly at law faculties in Europe and elsewhere. Insight into the purpose of this activity and its accompanying method can help in ascertaining whether this approach is rightly criticized or not.

There is not one academic discipline that can do without a proper description of its research object. In physics, objects are usually described by a quantification of their characteristics and behaviour. In the study of history, the objects of study range from countries to persons to objects that are usually described in qualitative terms. In psychology, people's behaviour is studied and its description takes place on the basis of both statistical and qualitative data.

> Simon Schama's *The Embarrassment of Riches* (1987) provides a fine example of 'description' in the field of history. It uses a wide range of methods, including the cultural-historical and comparative method, and is written in a literary style, leading to a type of creative non-fiction that lies in between literature and scholarship. I mention this example because it shows how every description is subjective and to a large extent dependent on the person making the description. In the field of the humanities, it is usually not the dry summarization of facts or data that is valued, but rather the stylistically advanced presentation of facts in a story, which is also reflected in the appreciation of authors like Schama and Johan Huizinga.

A proper description of the research object is not possible without a shared disciplinary framework for what such a description should look like. Textbooks in many fields pay attention to this. Thus, physics employs a wide arsenal of symbols, terms and formulas to describe the physical reality. In psychology, description usually takes place in both quantitative and qualitative terms. History studies employ a wide range of different methods.

> An accurate description of what is observed is of paramount importance in physics: the attempt to explain the observations comes only after an accurate description has been established. For example, see, for (usually mathematical) description, Riley & Hobson (2006). See, for psychology (in which description – through case studies or surveys – stands next to the experimental method and the method to correlate phenomena with each other), Shaughnessy et al. (2011), for example. Studies in fields such as history or literature have witnessed an extensive level of debate about methodology since the 1970s. In addition to textual analysis and comparative methods, literature studies have since added empirical studies to their methodology. See Guerin et al. (2010) for more details.

7. Description: The Doctrinal Approach

This survey of how description takes place in other fields forms the background to how law can be described. In the remainder of this section, I will first discuss the usual way of describing the positive law (nos. 7–10) and will subsequently go into several alternative approaches (nos. 11–15).

Descriptive legal science is usually equated with a doctrinal, black letter or dogmatic approach. The usual aim of this type of description is to present the law in a certain field (such as contract law or administrative law) in a way that is as neutral and consistent as possible in order to inform the reader how it actually reads. Examples of this include the description of German private law in the *Münchener Kommentar zum Bürgerlichen Gesetzbuch*, of English constitutional law in Dicey's *An Introduction to the Law of the Constitution* and of American law in the big treatises. Von Savigny's monumental *System of the Modern Roman Law* (1840–1848 [1979]) also belongs to this type of scholarship. They are all informed by a desire to place the prevalent sources of law (including legislation and case law) in a system and to develop this system further.

The examples given make it clear that it would be wrong to identify this approach as non-creative. Descriptive legal science, to the contrary, requires many choices to be made, from the selection and the interpretation of the materials to the way in which the materials are presented. Jeremy Bentham was right when he designated this type of academic work as 'expository jurisprudence' (as opposed to 'censorial jurisprudence', dealing with the question of how the law ought to read). The term 'expository' accurately indicates that this description, as with any presentation, requires the making of choices and the proper elaboration of these choices.

See Bentham (1789, [1970 Ch. XVII, 21]). Twining (1994, 123, 131ff.) also mentions Blackstone's *Commentaries* as an important example of the expository tradition in law and rightly emphasizes that 'even the lowest forms of exposition involve interpretation, selection and arrangement of quite elusive data'. Also, the preparation of restatements of law (such as those published by the American Law Institute (ALI)) and of the principles of European private law (as in the European Civil Code project) may seem only to serve to describe what already exists (for the sake of simplification, as the ALI explicitly aims to do) but, in practice, the formulation of restatements requires many normative decisions, such as deciding which specificities of the jurisdictions involved are to be left out and which are to be elevated to general principles. This is because the sources will almost always contradict each other. In this respect legal academics do not differ from historians: as historians who claim to describe the historical reality in fact *make* history, legal academics lay down what is the applicable law. This does not mean that each description is as original as one would wish for. The coherent presentation of new materials or the categorization of old materials on the basis of new criteria require much more brainpower than the mere accommodation of recent legislation and judicial decisions in the existing system. If legal scholarship were fairly criticized for doing only the latter (which is, in my view, less and less the case), this would be merited: jurists employed by universities should be more ambitious than only to want to fit new materials into an existing framework (cf. *infra*, no. 8).

Until recently, the ability to do this type of traditional expository work was seen as the best method to distinguish good lawyers from bad ones, although arguably some aspects of this thought still persist in many countries around the world. This is not surprising: Rubin rightly points out that if the predominant way of thinking about law is a positivist one, or is based on some idea of natural law, describing the existing law in terms of underlying principles or rules forms the only real legal science. According to this particular view of the law as a system, the emphasis lies on description and legal scholars should refrain from making normative statements about how the law *should* be.

See Rubin (1996, 565): 'the comprehensive treatise was regarded as the apogee of scholarly attainment'. This type of work is sometimes qualified as *recherches ponctuelles* (in contrast to *recherches sublimes*; cf. Twining (1994, 125).

A well-known advocate of this type of legal formalism, and hence of the internal perspective on law and the systematizing method, is Ernest J. Weinrib (1995, 339–340). Weinrib emphasizes that formalism presupposes a view of law as an 'immanently intelligible normative practice'. This means that a legal system is already justified by its own coherence but will have to be permanently readjusted on the basis of new judicial decisions and legislation: 'Justificatory coherence points not outward to a transcendent ideal but inward to a harmonious interrelationship among the constituents of the structure of justification'. From a different perspective, Ronald Dworkin (1986) also points out the great importance of this type of coherence. See, on the value of a doctrinal approach, also *infra*, no. 45.

There are two aspects of this type of description of law that have to be worked out: the way in which this description through systematization really takes place (the method) (nos. 8–9), and the inevitably internal perspective that the system builder has to adopt (no. 10).

8. Systematization

Which method is used if the law is described as a system? It seems useful to distinguish between the creation of a system and the accommodation of new elements within this system. This distinction is important because once a system is put into place and accepted by the legal community, creating a new *status quo*, it will influence the substantive law in the sense that deviating from it would prove to be difficult.

To create a system on virgin territory is without a doubt a highly creative activity. Presenting the law as a coherent set of concepts, rules and principles by exposing contradictions, defining concepts and classifying rules and cases, has defined the history of legal scholarship. The well-known Dutch law professor and drafter of the new Dutch Civil Code, Eduard M. Meijers, described this as the 'dogmatic method': the scholarly cultivation of legal norms or principles on basis of the laws of logic: 'One takes a certain set of law matter as given and then tries to make this more complete in form and substance without using any other empirical knowledge'.

This systematizing method comes close to what is common in the natural sciences: the existing materials (produced by legislatures, courts and others) are described in order to make them easier for readers to understand, and also to make their outcomes more predictable. These legal descriptions thus make it easier for readers to criticize existing materials and to analyse their impact in a similar manner to the way the laws of natural science can be exposed and criticized on the basis of an observation of facts. Cicero was already describing this working method when he answered Catullus's question on how to comprehend the interminable and immense amount of law:

> 'These matters Crassus will one day disentangle for us and set forth arranged under heads; for you must know, Catullus, that yesterday he promised us that he would collect under definite heads the common law, at present dispersed in disorder, and would reduce it to an easy system.'

However, it was not until the sixteenth century before, under the influence of humanism and natural law, and parallel to a similar development in other fields, a legal *mos geometricus* came into existence.

Meijers (1903, 14, 19). It is well known that almost any form of systematization of law was absent in Roman times (see for the citation of Cicero: De Oratore (55 BC [1942 II, xxxiii]). It was through the works of authors like Hugo Donellus (1527–1591) and Jean Domat (1625–1696) that the mass of amorphous rules was systematized into a new legal science, 'just as scientific, just as dependable and just as certain as the natural sciences of Newton and Copernicus' (Van der Walt 1995, 402). However, it lasted until the nineteenth century before the axiomatic systematization of the whole of private law was achieved in the form of the apogee of legal rationality: Von Savigny's *System of the Modern Roman Law* (1840–1848 [1979]). In this eight-volume work, all rules found their proper place in the system by way of the

> empirical-deductive method. It led to abstractions such as the legal act (*Rechtsgeschäft*) and a general theory of contract law. Von Savigny himself rightly compared his method to that of mathematics: 'In every triangle (. . .) there are certain data from the relations of which all the rest are necessarily deducible: thus (. . .) the whole triangle is given. In like manner, every part of our law has points by which the rest may be given. These may be termed the leading axioms. To distinguish these, and deduce from them the internal connection, and the precise degree of affinity which subsists between all juridical notions and rules, is amongst the most difficult of the problems of jurisprudence. Indeed, it is peculiarly this which gives our labours the scientific character' (Von Savigny 1814 [1831, 38–39]).

More recent examples of the systematization of fields that had until then been uncharted territory are provided by the 'discovery' of the reliance principle by the German author Claus-Wilhelm Canaris (1971), the systematization of new types of contract by Michael Martinek (1991–1993) and the description of the English law of restitution by Peter Birks (1985).

> It may seem surprising that even Richard Posner (2007, 437) recognizes the great importance of this type of academic work: 'The messy work product of the judges and legislators requires a good deal of tidying up, of synthesis, analysis, restatement, and critique. These are intellectually demanding tasks, requiring vast knowledge and the ability (not only brains and knowledge and judgment, but also *Sitzfleisch*) to organize dispersed, fragmentary, prolix, and rebarbative materials. These are tasks that lack the theoretical breadth or ambition of scholarship in more typically academic fields. Yet they are of inestimable importance to the legal system and of greater social value than much esoteric interdisciplinary legal scholarship.' Cf., however, *infra*, no. 50.

9. Normative Consequences of Systematization

It is important to realise that once a legal system is put in place – no matter how coincidental its structure may be – this system will, to a large extent, determine the outcome of future descriptions. True, legal academics will always be able to produce wholly new legal conceptions and distinctions, but this is usually not seen as very fruitful. In the European-continental tradition, there is a programmatic desire to continue the systematization on the basis of the existing legal system. This means that new rules and cases will almost always be fitted into the existing categorizations.

See Rothacker (1954) and Smits (2002a). This does not mean that the accommodation of new materials does not also contribute to the creation of a system. Legal systems are dynamic: they need to be worked on permanently in the light of the new materials that are produced. However, this always happens within the limits of the system itself: the law is conservative in nature in order to be able to meet the requirements of legal certainty and equality.

One aspect of this systematization needs to be highlighted. Legal systematization differs in one important respect from description in other disciplines – it influences the application of the law in practice. Because legal academics work on a system that is also used in practice, important normative consequences can follow from this work. This makes the description of law always normative, even if the person describing it is not aware of it. Anyone making use of a coherent system will propagate a change of the law if this fits in with the system itself. Koopmans describes this as follows:

'If biologists classify a whale as a mammal instead of as a fish, nothing changes in the world of facts (. . .). But if jurists qualify a barstool as a movable object and not as an immovable, they mean to say that in case of insolvency of the pub owner, it is not the bank that as mortgagee is entitled to the stool, but the brewery (. . .).'

Any decision to systematize the law in a certain way can thus have practical consequences. At least in the continental legal tradition, legal science itself can *create* law.

Koopmans (1991, 68). The idea that positive law can be found by academic activity is the product of the nineteenth century. In the natural law tradition of authors like Samuel Pufendorf, the academic activity only consisted of classifying what was law already. This changed with the emergence of the *Begriffsjurisprudenz*, leading to the system being a source of law itself. Schröder (2001, 245) puts it like this: 'Im 19. Jahrhundert dehnt sie ihre Kompetenz auf den Stoff selbst aus' due to the Kantian idea that our knowledge is not dependent on the objective reality, but the other way around: objects are the result of our knowledge. This opened up the way for an independent legal science that developed an 'inner system'. See also Feinman (1989, 663): 'how we think about law' and 'the law we think about' are not two different things: 'Definition creates reality as much as it orders it.'

The distinction between describing the law and giving a normative judgment about how the law should read is not always made in a clear way. Statements about optimal law are often given by way of an interpretation of an existing statute or judicial decision. In so far as courts engage in this practice, this is – at least in civil law jurisdictions – understandable from their fear to create new law: they would rather cover this up. When legal academics mimic this practice, however, their actions should be discouraged.

It should be emphasized that the systematizing method leaves open the option of deciding which materials, exactly, are to be systematized. Until the nineteenth century, this was mostly Roman law, whereas today systematization is mostly based on the products of national legislatures and courts. This is remarkable, considering that the method of 'finding' a system in the mass of judicial decisions and statutes was originally directed towards the creation of a universal legal science: just as a 'national physics' could not exist so knowledge of different national laws was only a means to establish a universal discipline.

At present, we have as many legal systems as countries. It is only because of their common historical roots that these jurisdictions resemble each other. See, for example, on the idea of a universal legal science, Schweber (1999). From the viewpoint of the requirements that an academic discipline (including the legal discipline) should meet, it is problematic to look at *national* materials only (and even more so if one looks exclusively at the products of the legislature and courts): see *infra*, nos. 21 and 39. A more original approach is one that also takes into account private regulation and rules flowing from European and international lawmakers (cf. *infra*, no. 25) in describing the applicable law – as it, for example, takes place in the 'global administrative law' movement.

10. An Internal Perspective

The second aspect of the traditional description of law is that it usually takes place from an *internal* perspective. The biologist describing the behaviour of the hedgehog does so in his own scientific language and not in that of the hedgehog itself, just like the sociologist studying the medical profession does not have to be an expert in medical jargon. The literary critic, also, does not aim to become a writer himself (at least not in most cases). The legal academic, however, makes use of exactly the same legal terminology as the object of his study. And this is not all. Rubin (using a term of Foucault's) defines this as the 'unity of discourse': legal scholars 'not only analyse the work of judges, but they also tend to think of themselves as judges, and to speak like judges. They address a court on the court's own terms, offering alternative rationales for the decision reached, or arguments why a different decision was preferable.'

Rubin (1988, 1859ff.). This phenomenon was extensively discussed in the American literature. Learned Hand (1926, 466) described jurists and judges as 'laborers in the same vineyard'. And what Posner (2002, 1315) stated with regard to American legal academics well into the 1970s is still accurate for their European counterparts: 'They even dressed like lawyers rather than like professors. They passed easily between the university and non-academic venues such as the courtroom and the government agency.' For an account of the close relationship between law-making and learning in Germany: Vogenauer (2006).

This perspective of the participant is also an inherent part of the training of law students: much of the legal curriculum is meant to put students in the position of a judge, legislator, lawyer or counsel and in fact to *make a decision*. This perspective of the legal academic as involved in the legal process itself has for a long time been seen as invariably positive. Weinrib even sees the internal perspective as what makes legal scholarship an autonomous discipline: as soon as it adopts an external (economic, sociological, historical, etc.) perspective, there is no longer a legal approach to the problem in question.

> This implies that the legal academic has to *find* law himself. See Weinrib (1995) and Rubin (1996, 562). It is through this internal perspective that legal science and practice are closely related: someone whose aim in life is to indicate how the law reads or ought to read, lends a ready ear to those who have to apply the law.

This internal perspective fits in with the general insight that an adequate description of the research object is generally given by a researcher who puts himself in the position of the participant. This participant observation is well known from the field of anthropology. However, the question must be asked whether – in the case of law – this prevailing view does not focus too much on the insider's perspective (see *infra*, no. 25).

11. Description in Legal Science: Alternative Approaches

Can description of law also take place in other ways than through doctrinal analysis? It is beyond doubt that the answer must be affirmative: there are many examples of such an *external* description of jurisdictions, that is, a description that takes place in other terms than those of the jurisdiction itself. This type of description usually makes use of the methods of other disciplines, including sociology, anthropology and economics. Comparative law and legal history do seem to make use of legal terminology when they describe foreign or past jurisdictions, but this is due to the way in which these disciplines are usually practised, namely as *legal* disciplines (that is to say from an internal perspective) and not as an exponent of the comparative or historical method. I briefly pay attention to these other types of description.

This survey can be brief because it is not essential to the main argument developed in this book. I also acknowledge that sociologists, economists and historians may not fully recognize their work in this necessary limited sketch. In no. 40, *infra*, yet another type of description is presented: because of increasing Europeanization of law, there is an increasing need for description not in terms of rules, but by way of arguments.

12. Sociological Description of Law

Since Eugen Ehrlich published his famous *Fundamental Principles of the Sociology of Law* (1913 [1936]), it has been clear that the law can be described from a sociological perspective as well as in terms of doctrine. After Ehrlich, it was Max Weber who, in *Economy and Society* (1922 [1946]), distinguished between a description in legal terms and a more value-free description from an external perspective. To Weber, this was a description in rather abstract terms. Thus, one can describe law in terms of the values it tries to realize (such as the limitation of state power), in terms of the relationship between the normative (the aspiration) and the factual (how this aspiration works out in practice) or as a demonstration of class interests. The description of law as governance, which considers law as a way to exercise power in a legitimate and coherent manner is also prominent.

See Weber (1922 [1968]). Llewellyn (1930, 3) described law in terms of dispute resolution: law is 'what (. . .) officials do about disputes'. On law as governance see, instead of many, Hunt & Wickham (1994, 99ff.). Legal realism also aims at a description of how law 'really' works. Holmes approached this from the perspective of 'decision analysis': the question is how decisions about law are taken in practice. This puts the 'bad man' at the centre of attention, who is only interested in how the judge will decide his case and bases his (from the moral perspective perhaps rather unedifying) behaviour on this. See Holmes (1897, 461): 'The prophecies of what the courts will do in fact, and nothing more pretentious, are what I mean by the law'. See for an overview of (American) legal realism: Leiter (1996). In the last decade, new approaches to legal realism have been proposed in the United States. This 'new legal realism' proposes to make use of more quantitative research methods and encourages legal academics to do more fieldwork. See, for example, the special issue of *Wisconsin Law Review* (2005, 335ff.) and the website <www.newlegalrealism.org>.

An important part of the sociology of law deals with the effects of rules on society. This type of research usually has a strong normative bias and investigates whether the (deficient) functioning of a rule should have consequences for its acceptance. In this regard, the study by sociologists is no longer a description of law, but actual empirical scholarship (see *infra*, no. 16).

13. Economic Description of Law

Law can also be described in terms of economic analysis. In the discipline of Law and Economics, it is common to distinguish between normative and descriptive (positive) analysis. In the (disputed) normative variant, economic analysis deals with the question of how the law ought to read (or how substantive disputes need to be decided) if it aims at maximizing welfare: legal rules are then to be designed in such a way that they will promote such welfare. An economic description of law only aims to describe and explain the *existing* law on the basis of economic principles. On this issue, Richard Posner observes that 'the common law is best explained as if courts were trying to maximise economic welfare'. If this is really the case, it shows that large parts of private law and criminal law can be understood as pursuing efficiency and have developed into systems of welfare maximization.

This approach is based on one of the most influential journal articles ever published: Coase (1960); also see Posner (1983, 4). Posner claims that the 'rhetoric of opinions' only leads to covering up the underlying reasons for a legal judgment. Instead, legal education and research should aim at uncovering the *true* reasons; efficiency then comes out as an important factor (Posner 2003, 25). There is thus an economic basis for tort liability, fair trial, compensation for expropriation and the principle against unjustified enrichment (Posner 2003, 27). Economic analysis may also reveal the adverse effects of consumer protection (Posner 2003, 27), which demonstrates how description can easily become a normative activity (on which *infra*, no. 34).

14. Historical Description of Law

One would expect legal historians and comparative lawyers to be experienced in describing the law. This is because they are supposed to struggle with the question of how past law or foreign law can be objectively presented because, at first blush, doing this in terms of present law does not suffice.

And yet, this is exactly the approach that most legal historians follow. The Dutch legal historian Henk Hoetink makes a distinction between a purely historical approach and a description on the basis of present-day law. The first approach aims to reproduce the law as it really was in order to reflect the historical reality that once existed. This means that the conceptions and rules of that time are placed in the broader cultural and economic context of the past. The second approach departs from present-day law, which it extends backwards in order to solve modern problems. In this scenario, history is used to draw lessons that are applicable to improving current law, not to seek the objective restoration of what once was. It is entirely plausible then that past law is not presented in an entirely correct way but this is of minor significance if we consider that a 'productive misunderstanding' can be immensely useful.

See Hoetink (1929 [1986, 27ff.): in the first approach, legal history is part of cultural history, a study that comes out of 'disinterested

> interest'. This purely historical study of law is closely associated with the names of Ranke and Mommsen, but modern examples of this approach include the works on American legal history written by Friedman (1973 [2005]) and Horwitz (1977). In practice, legal historians mainly use the second approach, where they describe jurisdictions primarily from an internal perspective. That is to say by using their *own* classifications, concepts and rules it makes them, above all, jurists and not historians. We find a similar debate in comparative legal studies, where a strictly academic approach would require the description of a foreign jurisdiction on its own terms. However, as comparison can also serve other purposes than just accumulating objective knowledge, other methods have come to the fore (cf. Husa 2009).

It is striking to see the near obliviousness or the general lack of awareness that many legal historians possess when it comes to acknowledging the existence of alternative methods available in the field of history when describing the past. This is a pity because legal history could profit from these views when describing the historical reality in law.

> Comparative lawyers also struggle with questions that similarly afflict legal historians. See, for example, the overview by Ankersmit (2001). Historical description also requires the making of choices, which becomes evident in the debate about the extent to which there is one European civil law tradition. While Zimmermann, in *The Law of Obligations* (1990), emphasizes the continuity of this tradition, Monateri (2000) is much more sceptical and sees mostly rifts in history and a discontinuous development of Roman law to modern law. This is a matter of perspective: one sees continuity when identifying a rule that one is liable for selling a defective product but discontinuity if this product is a slave in Roman times and a MacBook in the present.

15. Comparative Description of Law

An identical question ('How to describe another law than one's own?') is discussed among comparative lawyers. Again, one can distinguish between a description in terms of a foreign jurisdiction and one in terms of one's own legal system. Comparatists, unlike legal historians, quarrel to no end about what is the best approach.

Describing a jurisdiction in the context of that jurisdiction itself is usually not seen as very problematic since most comparative work is directed to comparisons of similar legal systems within the same legal family. In such cases, the foreign terminology is usually similar to that of one's own system. Even if a term has a different meaning elsewhere, it will not be fundamentally different from the meaning attached to it in its own jurisdiction so one does not need a truly external viewpoint in order to understand the foreign jurisdiction.

A well-known exception to this is so-called 'false friends' (terms that look identical, but actually have a wholly different meaning) (see Tallon (1998)).

Things change quickly when foreign law cannot be captured in terms of one's own jurisdiction. Comparative literature then usually turns to the so-called functional method: which (societal) function does the legal rule or even the legal system as a whole have? Different legal rules and legal systems are then compared by choosing a standard of measurement that is external to the law.

A famous example of functional description at the micro level is the article by Konrad Zweigert (1964) about indicia of seriousness in contract law, where the question is which rules are used to distinguish binding from non-binding promises. It is only from this functional perspective that one is able to relate *causa*, consideration, and the intention to create legal relationships. It is probably true that the more diverse legal systems are, the more abstract the measure of comparison has to be. Thus, anthropologist Von Benda-Beckmann (1979) distinguishes all law in terms of variations on a general category. This variation can be described in terms of the degree of institutionalization, of *mandatoriness*, and of restricting the autonomy of individuals. See also Strijbosch (1996, 536). The description of law in terms of so-called 'law jobs' is also well known: each society has certain (legal) functions, such as deciding disputes, regulating behaviour, deciding who has authority, determining how such authority is to be exercised, and providing cohesion (this method was famously applied to the non-state law of the Cheyenne Indians by Llewellyn and Hoebel (1941)). Also see Hoebel (1967 [2006]).

Describing a foreign legal system in terms of one's own legal system is insofar a Dutch academic tradition that it also took place in the so-called '*Adat* school' of Cornelis van Vollenhoven and others. They aimed to codify the 'living law' of the peoples of the Indonesian archipelago in non-Western terminology. Thus, this people's own conception of their 'native law' (as opposed to the academic description of it in the terms of the lawyer) was emphasized. Van Vollenhoven spoke of 'seeing oriental law in the oriental way'. See Holleman (1981). There was even a manual for recording the law in Indonesia, the so-called *Adat Guide* (1910), prescribing the method of research and describing the law. In line with his own method, Van Vollenhoven distinguished nineteen areas of law (*rechtskringen*) in the archipelago by way of 'neutral' neologisms, explicitly avoiding, for example, the distinction between property law and the law of obligations, and by using terms such as land law (*for example,* 'tenancy in return for loan' or *grondverpanding*) and the law of wrongs (thus avoiding the distinction – unknown to *Adat* law – between acts that are criminally punishable and civil law torts).

The question must be raised whether this functional method is truly the best way to compare jurisdictions. Describing a law by way of reference to non-legal concepts risks the possibility that the reader fails to capture the essence of that law (and what it means to those affected by it).

Nils Jansen draws an important parallel with the study of (comparative) religion. This discipline suffers from an identical problem as comparative legal science: how to describe (the conceptions of) a religion in an objective fashion? How, for example, does one describe a term like 'holiness' or compare the diverse views about 'God'? The personal opinion of the person describing the subject cannot be decisive and neither can a functional approach: to look at religious commandments or view the resurrection of Christ as functional problems seems to miss the heart of what a religion is about (Jansen 2006, 328). And yet, a comparison is possible by describing a phenomenon existing in different religions as a common phenomenon, and subsequently analysing the commonalities and differences inherent in it. This means that comparison takes place by way of a 'comparative second-order language', which is an inter-subjective description that allows one to decide from the 'inside out' what is and is not important. This approach can also be of service in legal comparison: see *infra*, no. 46 and, for further criticism of functionalism, Husa (2003).

3. EMPIRICAL LEGAL SCHOLARSHIP

16. Research on the Effects of Law

A second type of legal science, known as empirical legal science, is not directed towards a (doctrinal or other) description of law, but deals with its application and consequences. Empirical legal science studies the legal actors, institutions, rules and procedures in order to obtain a better understanding of how they operate and what effects they have. This field is therefore not about what the law says, but about what it *does*. This type of work is becoming increasingly popular, partly caused by the view that 'real' knowledge must be empirically testable.

For the above definition, see Baldwin & Davis (2003, 881). Ellickson (2000) demonstrates the extent to which, in the United States, the number of studies at the intersection of law and other disciplines has increased in the last twenty years. For the period 1985–2000, Korobkin (2002) counts 27 articles in American law journals using an empirical approach to the law of contract. This number has increased substantially since then: there are now also law journals entirely devoted to an empirical approach, such as the *Journal of Legal Studies*, the *Law and Society Review*, the *Journal of Law and Society* and the *Journal of Empirical Legal Studies*. Heise (2002) provides a history of empirical legal scholarship.

Attention to how a statute or judicial decision affects reality is a little surprising for today's jurists. The days of a purely doctrinal approach, in which a judgment about the value of a rule was only based on the extent to which it fitted into the doctrinal system – if those times ever existed at all – are now far behind us. One need not repeat the famous statement that, 'We are all realists now' to be aware of this.

This approach has its foundations in the work of Von Jhering, Ehrlich and Weber (see *supra*, no. 12) and in American legal realism. Louis Brandeis was one of the first to explain before the United States Supreme Court how a statute on the regulation of the working hours of women worked out in practice (*Muller* v. *Oregon*, 208 U.S. 412 (1908) and Roscoe Pound's *Social Control Through Law* of 1942 subsequently elaborated on this emphasis on 'law in action'. See extensively Stein (2000, 21) on the *Folgenanalyse* in Germany.

We must not, however, overestimate the importance of empirical work to the law. Holmes' famous saying that 'for the rational study of the law the black-letter man may be the man of the present, but the man of the future is the man of statistics and the master of economics' did not materialize. This is because the relationship between the normative question of what the law ought to be ('What is allowed in law and what is not?') and the empirical question of whether something 'works' is not completely clear. The premise of empirical research is that the law is an *instrument* and that it can therefore be tested in an empirical way. This implies a strongly instrumental view of law that is difficult to reconcile with a doctrinal approach. The tension between the two models of academic work becomes apparent when the construction of a logically coherent system of principles is in the driving seat and one that investigates empirical reality (in terms of cause and effect) takes a backseat.

See Holmes (1897, 469). In a doctrinal approach, there is no need for an empirical analysis. The only test is whether the rule fits in with the (coherent) system. This is different as soon as the societal effect of the law starts playing a role in assessing it. Ulen (2002, 27) mentions yet another reason: the traditionally marginal role of empirical research in law is also caused by the fact that law does not have a testable *core theory*. This is different in many other disciplines (such as economics with its emphasis on the rational actor). It should also be mentioned that the ever-increasing role of regulation by the state leads to a greater need for empirical research. If law is primarily used as a policy instrument to pursue certain goals, the empirical testing of the extent to which these goals are achieved is only one step away. See also *infra*, no. 35.

The empirical approach was originally strongly directed towards identifying factors that determine how judicial decisions come about. In contrast to doctrinal analysis, it was no longer seen to be decisive how the law reads, but a role was assigned to the judge in understanding why a decision was taken. Today, legal-empirical work is particularly strong in the fields of criminal law, labour law, environmental law and access to the legal profession.

Recently, much attention has been directed towards the consumers of legal services (Baldwin & Davis, 2003, 887) and towards negotiations. Perhaps the most talked-about exponent of the empirical approach in the last few years is the American, Steven Levitt, whose work is characterized by the motto that law and morals may be about how one would wish the world to work, but it is more important to know how the world works *de facto*. How this can lead to exceptionally stimulating research is shown by a much-debated article in which Levitt and Donahue look for an explanation for the reduction of crime in the United States after 1990. Their explanation is that the legalization of abortion by the United States Supreme Court in *Roe v. Wade* (410 U.S. 113 (1973)) led to fewer children being born who were unwanted by their parents. Since unwanted children are more likely to become criminals because not enough preparation is put in place for their upbringing, legalization of abortion would have led to less crime (Levitt & Donahue 2001).

Next to the very well established field of criminology, there is an increasing need for empirical testing of the regulation of private relationships. It has been noted more than once that a private law counterpart of criminology is largely missing or, as it was put in a report by the British *Nuffield Foundation* (2006): 'There is no "civilology" equivalent to criminology', hinting at the lack of comprehensive empirical work in fields such as family law, commercial law, labour law and contract law. The overview of types of research by Siems (2008) demonstrates how many kinds of legal-empirical research are possible and that it does not make much sense to lump them together. Research into the extent to which parties are aware of law (Ellickson 1991) makes a world of difference to research into ways of deciding conflicts (Genn 1999) and research into the question of whether common law jurisdictions are better for economic development than their civil law counterparts (Shleifer & Glaeser 2002; Faure & Smits 2011).

It does not come as a surprise that the empirical approach derives its methods from non-legal disciplines. Taking empirical research seriously requires using the methods of other disciplines rather than those of the law to find answers to the relevant questions. However, one cannot expect the same type of certainty from empirical legal research as, for example, natural science can offer: the results are simply less robust – which does not mean that these are therefore less important.

The usual distinction is the one between qualitative and quantitative empirical research methods. The former usually consists of conducting interviews, carrying out case studies or reading documents. The results of this type of research cannot always be generalized, but this does not matter so much because usually the aim is to understand a legal phenomenon better and not to collect empirical evidence for the sake of collecting data. The quantitative method can consist of a large-scale collection of data and the application of statistical analysis to it, as often happens in criminology and victimology. It is also possible to carry out an experiment, as Hesen (2009, 147ff.) recently did, where she investigated the cognitive load of contracts by having 120 students answer questions about almost 400 contracts in the biopharmaceutical sector.

Baldwin & Davis (2003, 889ff.) show well that empirical research in law is often not very thorough when compared to, for example, political science or psychology: 'Research skills are picked up by observing more experienced colleagues, and there is nothing particularly complex or technical about the methods employed'. This is not much of a problem as the results are often plausible and influential. Thus, the famous work of Macaulay (1963) on the actual use of contract law by business people is based on a relatively small number of interviews. Also, see *infra*, no. 55 for putting the robustness of empirical data into perspective when used in legal studies.

4. THE THEORETICAL PERSPECTIVE

17. Research about Law

Next to descriptive and empirical legal scholarship, there is still a third type of legal research that can be distinguished. This is research about the question of what is law, in what does the law differ from other sets of rules, why and when is it valid, and how does it develop. Philosophy of law and legal theory traditionally deal with these questions, but questions about the law are often also raised in other sub-disciplines. This meta-legal perspective is only discussed briefly here.

This type of research is certainly not limited to the elevated questions that philosophy of law deals with and that are brilliantly described by Bix (2009). Questions about the optimal design of private law (Purnhagen 2013), about the need for a uniform European private law (Smits 2005) and about the influence of the late Spanish scholastics on Hugo Grotius' views about mistake and unjustified enrichment (Feenstra 1974) also belong to this category.

The term 'meta-legal' perspective is often used to describe all approaches that are not doctrinal, thus also covering fields such as Law and Psychology, Sociology of Law and Law and Economics. However, these topics are often more directly related to the positive law, that is then looked at from the perspective of a specific method.

The enormous value of the theoretical perspective is that it usually does not start from the subdivisions of substantive fields of law, but tries to acquire insights relevant to various legal areas. The challenge then is to remain informed about developments in these specific fields and to make the acquired general insights accessible again to specialists, which is no easy task. Thus, the present challenge seems to be to find a new philosophical foundation for law in times of increasing internationalization of law. There is a dire need for a new legitimation of law, which will accommodate other legal sources than those that fit in with a positivist view, where the growing Europeanization and privatization of law make it increasingly difficult to determine what is law by making use of criteria such as Kelsen's *Grundnorm* or Hart's *rule of recognition*.

See *supra*, nos. 27 and 40. There is an extensive literature on the consequences of internationalization for conceptions such as the rule of law, democracy and sovereignty. In the fields of European private law or European constitutional law, the discussion is also extensive, but deals mainly with the *substance* of European norms and with the influence they have on national law. A more extensive theory of how Europeanization leads to a whole new category of 'law beyond the State' and how this influences substantive fields is largely missing. An inventory of the literature is provided by Michaels & Jansen (2006), Jansen & Michaels (2007); also see De Burca (2008). For example, the question of the level at which laws are best regulated, whether it be at the local, the national, the European, or even at the supranational level was not addressed until the enormous increase in Europeanization, not to mention the alternate possibility that regulation ought to be left in the hands of the private sector. The answer to this question also determines how the systematization of private law is to take place: by way of making one European system or as separate national and European systems that each have their own rationality (on which Michaels 2011).

Theoretical work can make use of a variety of methods. Philosophy of law and legal theory tend to make use of the same methods and techniques of argumentation as in the more positive fields of law. The research question often also invites us to make use of methods (and insights) from other disciplines.

> In particular, theoretical work can profit from the ways other disciplines approach certain questions. Thus, when asking how a legal system develops, inspiration can be derived from evolutionary theory, and when asking whether the unification of law is needed, an economic approach can be useful (see respectively, Smits 2002b and 2005).

5. WHAT IS NEXT?

18. Continuing the Debate

Three important approaches to doing legal research were discussed above. Legal academics can describe law, can ask how law works in society, and can deal with theoretical questions about the nature and development of law. Each of these activities is useful and has its own methods. However, there is still a fourth approach to law: as already indicated, *supra* (no. 4), legal academics can also raise the normative question of what the law ought to be. This is, in my view, at the core of the legal discipline and therefore deserves to be discussed separately. The subsequent Chapters II and III are devoted to this type of research.

II. The *Homo juridicus*: towards a redefinition of normative legal science

1. INTRODUCTION

19. Course of the Argument

The introduction to this book showed that there is much work to be done pertaining to the aims and methods of legal science, the impact of which has reached a point where legal academics themselves can no longer distinguish the core of their activity. This is why, in Chapter I, four questions about the law were identified to facilitate legal academics in classifying their research. This should not make us forget, however, what is at the core of the legal discipline. The main thesis of this book is that legal science is primarily formed by the question of how the law *ought* to read. Before elaborating on this point further, this chapter will investigate the requirements that an academic discipline should meet in general (nos. 20–22). Normative legal science is then identified as the core of the legal discipline in nos. 23–26, followed by an account of what could be the theoretical underpinning of this view (nos. 27–29).

2. WHAT MAKES AN ACADEMIC DISCIPLINE?

20. Academic Disciplines

Needless to say, not all academic disciplines are similar. This is why the various branches of scholarship are usually distinguished on the basis of their characteristics and methods. Thus, the formal (or *a priori*) sciences are usually contrasted with the empirical sciences. Formal sciences (such as mathematics, logic and computer science) study abstract objects starting from certain existing axioms and rules of inference. The validity of a theory is then completely dependent on these axioms: the reality they create is a wholly artificial one. This is fundamentally different in empirical sciences (such as physics and biology): here, the validity of a theory can be tested by way of physical experiment. A third type of discipline is formed by the humanities, dealing with the diverse products of the human mind.

See, for example, Salmon (1999) and Leezenberg & De Vries (2001). Other distinctions within the empirical sciences concern the experimental (physics), observational (astronomy) and interpretative (several subfields of psychology) disciplines. The humanities often do not aim to find *the* truth or new facts, but usually search for an alternative perspective on existing facts, not necessarily leading to the elimination of existing perspectives.

Other distinctions within science are also possible, ranging from the age-old to very modern ones. Aristotle already distinguished between theoretical sciences (aiming to obtain 'pure' knowledge, such as in philosophy), practical sciences (which is about the actions of citizens – law, ethics and political science) and poetical disciplines (pursuing knowledge about making things). National organizations for scientific research (such as the Dutch Nederlandse Organisatie voor Wetenschappelijk Onderzoek and the German Deutsche Forschungsgemeinschaft) often lump together the various social sciences (including law, economics and psychology); cf. *infra*, no. 53). Another distinction is the one between 'pure' science (such as theoretical physics) and applied disciplines (such as mechanical engineering and medicine).

In this context, there is much debate over the question of how to categorize the legal discipline within the various branches of scholarship. In my view, this is completely dependent on the aim one pursues when studying law: this can make law not only part of the humanities, but can also mean it has to be categorized as an empirical or normative discipline.

> The legal discipline belongs to the humanities in so far as it emphasizes that the doctrinal system ('dogmatics') and the formulations of norms are products of the human mind. The accompanying research method is then in many cases the hermeneutical one. Law is also an empirical discipline in so far as it deals with how rules work in practice (see *supra*, no. 16). In an extreme variant of this, we can only accept as law what 'works' (see also *infra*, no. 35). One can even defend the proposition that legal norms undergo a similar development to the laws of nature: it may be that legal norms cannot be determined by way of induction and generalization, but that they have to be accepted in society. Looked at it in this way, norms are only hypotheses that become valid by their application to the facts (see for example, Engisch (1977) and *infra*, no. 52). Finally, law can also be a *normative* discipline (see *infra*, Section 3).

Determining which of the three variants we are dealing with is irrelevant when answering the question which requirements the legal discipline should meet in order to qualify as an academic discipline. The requirements we want an academic discipline to meet are independent of the classification of these variants.

21. Requirements of an Academic Discipline

The academic disciplines that were just distinguished, no matter how diverse they are, have several things in common. If a discipline is to be seen as an academic one, it must meet certain requirements. First, all scholarly disciplines aim for the systematization of knowledge: they are not satisfied with a loose collection of data, but aim to describe, evaluate and explain information within an existing framework. Secondly, this knowledge must have been obtained by a method that is recognized as valid by the academic community. Thirdly, all disciplines aim for knowledge that supersedes the local:

academic work aims for *universal* knowledge and is therefore necessarily international.

See for example Ruane (2005, 10ff.). It is not only (natural) science that aims for the systematization of knowledge; this is true for any academic discipline. The term 'scientia' refers to knowledge; and knowledge seems impossible without reference to a number of ordered elements. Hence, the Oxford English Dictionary describes science as a branch of study that is concerned with 'a connected body of demonstrated truths or with observed facts systematically classified (. . .)'.

The subsequent requirement is that knowledge is either obtained through a recognized research method or is at least recognized as part of an academic practice. This methodological requirement finds its origins in the fact that the knowledge obtained has to be reliable and not based only on an intuition or a feeling: use of an accepted method can thus make the knowledge more objective and minimize the chance of mistake. This does not mean that the method is the same for every discipline. In the natural sciences, the method usually consists of an empirical observation of reality, even though this may not be a guarantee of finding 'objective' knowledge. The well known criticism by authors such as Gadamer (1960[1981], Habermas (1968[1987]) and MacIntyre (1981) is that an academic discipline can never offer an objective truth, but is at best a *practice*: a set of forms of argumentation recognized as valid by some academic community (cf. Rubin 1988, 1841). Whereas a method offers fixed rules to reach a certain (often replicable) result, a practice is based on judgments and sometimes even on intuition. The legal discipline has almost always been seen as such a practice, which also explains the relatively low importance that is attached to using clear research methods in academic work. As Rubin (1988, 1859) put it, law is a 'practice based on judgment, not on methodology based upon objectively determined rules'. Also see *infra*, no. 54.

Finally, academic disciplines aim at generalization. Despite differences between various fields – well known in this respect is the distinction Rickert makes between generalizing sciences (such as physics) and individualizing disciplines (such as history) – no field can limit itself to describing the here and the now: facts always

> have to be placed in a broader context in which national borders and language are not decisive.

Sometimes a fourth requirement is added to these three: the results must be replicable. This means that by using the same research method, a similar result must be reached. However, this is not an absolute requirement in all disciplines.

> Even in the natural sciences, the requirement of replicable results is no longer as important as it used to be. In fields like quantum mechanics and chaos theory, results are often unpredictable anyway and it is generally recognized that even in the 'hard' fields, knowledge is the result of a discourse in which rhetorical strategies play an important role. See, for example, Latour (1987). Outside natural science, the requirement of replication has never been that important. In his famous lecture, *The Two Cultures* of 1959 [1993], C.P. Snow was already arguing that important differences exist between disciplines and that one should not try to transplant the requirements of one discipline into another.

22. Requirements of (Descriptive) Legal Science

There is little doubt that the legal discipline can meet the three requirements that were discussed above. How these requirements work through is dependent on the type of legal science that is at stake: the descriptive, empirical and theoretical approaches will all make their own interpretation of the three universal academic requirements. It seems logical that the empirical and theoretical approaches cadge from the disciplines they originate from. But descriptive legal science can also meet the requirements needed to be considered academic.

This is beyond doubt, in so far as systematization and generalization are concerned. Existing law is pre-eminently described by way of the systematization of (usually) legislation and case law. This systematization is aimed at distinguishing the aspects of legislation and case law that have a more general importance from the less important details.

This type of systematization is not only a matter of course in private law, but also in other fields. See *supra*, no. 7. A methodological foundation of systematization is offered by for example Bydlinski (2003) and Wilburg (1950); also see *infra*, no. 55. However, the legal discipline differs from other fields in its emphasis on the systematization and generalization of *local* knowledge: the information that is to be systematized is usually confined to national borders. This is understandable in so far as one wants to describe national law. As soon as one's ambition reaches further, this restriction is no longer justified (such as deciding about what is desirable law, as is the case in normative legal scholarship: see *infra*, no. 25 and 48.

Legal science can also meet the requirement that knowledge is obtained through a method that the academic community recognizes as valid. Rubin rightly describes the legal discipline as 'a practice whose discourse consists largely of prescriptions that scholars address to public decision-makers for the purpose of persuading those decision-makers to adopt specified courses of action'. This general description of the legal discipline as a whole does not preclude the possibility that the descriptive variant has its own methods.

See Rubin (1988, 1881) and *infra*, no. 54. Description of law usually takes place by way of commonly accepted methods. In the doctrinal approach this is the empirical-deductive method as described earlier (no. 8). In the case of the alternative approaches described in nos. 12–15, one ideally consults sociology, economics or history to derive one's methods.

There are various reasons why the requirement that results should be replicable is not usually an issue in the legal field. The most important reason is that, in law, the value judgments of the researcher are often decisive for the result. In other words, the objectivity of natural science is not available because of the indeterminate nature of law.

Baldwin & Davis (2003, 891) rightly emphasize that 'there is little enthusiasm for re-testing a "finding" which everyone understands to be subjective to some degree'. See *infra*, nos. 50ff for a discussion of what this means for the 'innovativeness' of legal science and the extent to which legal knowledge is accumulated.

3. NORMATIVE LEGAL SCIENCE: IN SEARCH OF THE *HOMO JURIDICUS*

23. The Legal Perspective

In Chapter I, various academic approaches to the law were distinguished. As stated then, the core of legal science is formed by the normative question of what the law ought to be. The descriptive, empirical and theoretical approaches to law, which were previously distinguished, are no doubt prominent perspectives – and the latter two have rightly received a lot of attention lately – but this should not lead us away from the core of the legal discipline and how it differs from other fields.

In my view, the ultimate question of legal science is what the law *ought* to be: the legal discipline reflects upon what it is that individuals, firms, states and other organizations ought to do or ought to refrain from doing. Whilst the other three questions one can ask about law make use of a method that is also used in other disciplines (such as natural science, social science and philosophy), the search for the answer to this question is unique to the legal discipline. For example, should disinheriting one's children be permitted? Should a death penalty be imposed for criminal offences? Under what circumstances is it justified to go to war? Should constitutional review be allowed? Is it legitimate to discriminate in the private sphere? May shipwrecked sailors eat their weakest companion if they, themselves, are likely, otherwise, to die of starvation? To answer these and similar questions is *the* pre-eminently legal approach.

Because of the focus on this question, legal science is not dependent on the world of facts, or as Collier (1991, 271) rightly claims:

'The true realm and metier of legal scholarship (. . .) is the world of ideas'. It is not description (as in the natural and social sciences), interpretation (as in literature studies) or explanations of human behaviour (as in economics), but the normative question about what ought to be in law. Rubin (1988, 1847) speaks of the 'prescriptive voice' and the subtitle of the book by Michael Sandel (2009) on justice (*What's the Right Thing to Do?*) is also telling; cf. also Von Wright (1971). It is worth repeating in order to avoid misunderstanding – description, interpretation and explanation are most certainly part of legal science, but in my view they are not part of its normative core.

It is noticeable that this core of the legal discipline is only rarely made explicit. In every academic discipline, there are one or two core questions that every student can easily name. In physics, it is how to understand the physical reality, and in biology it is how living organisms function, grow and develop. Economists are also permanently aware of the fact that there is such a thing as the 'economic way of looking at life' (as Nobel Prize winner Gary Becker wrote) and of both the potential and the limits of this perspective. Lawyers usually lack such a clear vision of their field. This makes it necessary to re-evaluate normative legal science. While economists primarily study the behaviour of the *Homo economicus* (trying to explain human conduct from the economic perspective), lawyers try to answer a preceding question: what does it mean that a human being is a *Homo juridicus* and what is it, therefore, that he *ought* to do? This is as little related to what humans do *in fact* as it is in economics.

See Becker (1992): economists study the behaviour of *Homo economicus*, thus presuming that people and organizations behave rationally. Also see Heyne (2002, 4). In law, the premise is that actors *ought* to behave in the way required by law. Even Jeremy Bentham (1789 [1970]), who clearly distinguishes between descriptive and normative legal science, refrains from elaborating on what normative activity exactly comes down to being. The term 'Homo juridicus' was used before, but in a different context, by Supiot (2005). Hage (2011) explores whether a normative legal science is even possible.

24. Away from the Normative Haze

Perhaps the lack of focus on what is the core question of legal research can be explained by the phenomenon that, in traditional legal research, the description of existing law and the normative (and sometimes also the empirical) dimension are usually not clearly distinguished from each other. Often, academic work in law is geared to describing a piece of legislation or a judicial decision, followed by a discussion of whether the legislature or the court ruled correctly or incorrectly. The normative element is often camouflaged by interpreting the statute or decision in a certain way. This is a legitimate way of working in legal practice: it gives the impression that the law is subject to gradual and continuous development. However, this does not mean that both activities should not be separated analytically: from an academic perspective, a legal judgment by way of a 'reasonable' interpretation does not suffice. Any normative choice should not stay in the haze, but should be properly elucidated.

The type of questions practitioners are usually interested in is what is the *positive* law (as it exists here and today) as apparent from – usually – national legislation and case law. It may be that this positive law is not completely clear, leading to the question of how 'the law' should read. This question is then answered on the basis of the existing legal system, often by way of interpretation of existing (national) sources. See also Fletcher (1981, 987). There is nothing wrong with judges and practitioners answering a question in this way, but if academics do so, they make use of the internal approach towards law that is now under so much pressure. Rubin (1988, 1881) rightly observes: 'the process of justification is often better served by leaving the awkward unsaid and the incongruent unexplained, by generating a sort of normative haze in which implications drift about without coherent moorings'.

25. The Need for an External Normative Perspective

It may not seem very revolutionary to emphasize that the law is about the 'ought' and therefore deals with normative questions. However, it was noted above (no. 10) that legal academics often adopt an internal perspective: they use the same language and conceptions as their object of study and often have close ties with legal practice. We can now better understand why this is the case. The question of what the law ought to be is a question legal practice also deals with. It is because of the prescriptive nature of the legal discipline that academics make recommendations to those who decide what the law is, including to legislatures, courts and administrations using the same terms that the authorities use when formulating their commands.

This does not mean that this internal perspective is the only one that can be adopted in a normative approach to law. On the contrary, as soon as a distinction is made between the positive law (the whole body of authoritative statements about law at a certain place and time) and how the law ought to read, the internal perspective must be abandoned. The challenge is to develop such an external normative perspective. Legal science today is usually directed towards either the positive law or towards the non-normative (as in the empirical approach), so the blind spot seems to be the question of what *ought* to be.

> This approach distances itself from the view that the 'ought' is primarily decided by the competent authorities (in particular, the national legislatures and courts) or by what works empirically. The question is not what the legislature or court says, whether punishment achieves its goal, or whether awarding damages keeps a party from wrong behaviour in the future. These are no doubt relevant questions but how they are answered cannot be decisive for how the law should read. Also, see *infra*, no. 35.

There is every reason to develop this external normative perspective further. One of the reasons for this, as mentioned before (*supra*, no. 2), is that the critical approach to traditional legal scholarship threatens to create a situation where arguably only empirical or theoretical work can meet the highest standards of quality. This calls for a reorientation of the normative approach so as to satisfy the requirements of an academic discipline better.

This is because the criticism of the traditional (normative) way of doing legal research is partly justified: in so far as it is only oriented towards the products of the national legislature and courts, it does not meet the requirement for generalization (cf. *supra*, no. 22). This does not mean, however, that the entire normative approach should be banned for this reason – as Richard Posner (1990, 69) suggests: 'What is missing from law are penetrating and rigorous theories, counterintuitive hypotheses that are falsifiable but not falsified (. . .), precise instrumentation, an exact vocabulary, a clear separation of positive and normative inquiry, quantification of data, credible controlled experiments, rigorous statistical inference, useful technological byproducts, dramatic interventions with measurable consequences, and above all and subsuming most of the previous points, objectively testable – and continually retested – hypotheses'.

Another reason why an external normative perspective is required lies in the increasing Europeanization of law. Today's legal norms are no longer produced by national legislatures and courts only, but also flow from other sources. This should lead to a rethinking of the traditional relationship between the law and the state: the idea that law is primarily produced by democratically legitimized national institutions must be traded in for a view that better reflects today's reality. This means that legal science must look for an approach that determines what the law ought to be without making itself dependent on the authority of the official institutions, or of what empirically 'works'.

In the last 200 years, the standard view of law has been that law is 'made' by the democratic national institutions. European law is often only seen as a phenomenon that stands *next to* national law and most efforts are directed towards underpinning non-national law with conceptions of legitimacy that are derived from the state. In my opinion, this view no longer does justice to the complex reality of the law in a globalizing world. In the last few decades alone, European and international law-givers have not only produced a large numbers of norms, but private regulation also has become ubiquitous. All these different rules strongly influence the behaviour of individuals and organizations without being based in a national state.

There are countless examples of this 'global norm-production' (Teubner 1997, 157). Apart from organizations such as the IMF and the World Bank, the activities of the WTO in particular can have an important impact on the conduct of private parties, more specifically on the issues of free trade, taxes, intellectual property and protection of health. On the other hand, various types of voluntary law, such as norms adopted by corporate networks (the most important example being codes of conduct for corporate social or environmental responsibility), technical standards of standardization organizations (such as the 'codex alimentarius') and other types of self-regulation also influence the conduct of private parties. Of more recent origin are model rules such as the *Principles of European Contract Law* (PECL) and the Draft Common Frame of Reference for European Private Law (DCFR), on which *infra*, no. 41. They are primarily supposed to be a source of inspiration for (national and European) legislatures and courts.

Many of these norms, derived from 'sites of governance beyond the nation-state' (De Burca 2008, 104), would not be recognized as binding to a traditional conception of the law because they do not meet the formal criterion of being enacted by the relevant authorities and backed by coercive power. But they often do set the norms for specific groups of people and are therefore important in predicting their behaviour: in this sense, they are often more important as a source of private law than rules that are formally binding.

The conclusion to be drawn from this section is that, as the legitimacy of law was in the seventeenth and eighteenth century found in the laws of nature, and in the nineteenth and twentieth century it was founded on a democratic process of decision-making within national states, it is now time to find a new source of legitimacy for the twenty-first century (cf. *supra*, no. 17). See also Smits (2009a) and, for excellent overviews of the relationship between private law and the state, Michaels & Jansen (2006) and Jansen & Michaels (2007). As indicated, this book will primarily focus on one consequence of this development – how this new source of legitimacy will affect legal research. However, Section 4 of this chapter (nos. 27–28) attempts to find a theoretical underpinning of law that is not dependent for its validity on the official institutions.

26. Other Normative Disciplines

It should be pointed out that the legal discipline does not have the exclusive right of asking normative questions. Ethics (the discipline of formulating guidelines for the 'good life') is another field in which questions about the 'ought' are asked. Ethics, however, is not concerned with legal norms, but with norms of a moral nature (in which the sanction is not imposed by the state but by one's own conscience). These moral norms are usually formulated as commands of a general nature: 'Do not lie', 'Do good', 'Keep your promise', but – as is also the case in law – what these principles are worth can only be decided in an actual situation. Ethics also distinguishes between normative ethics ('What is the morally right thing to do?') and meta-ethics (in which this normative debate is analysed and the question can be asked, 'What are the origins of ethics?'). The least binding norms are social conventions: one does not text in the company of others, only runners are allowed to spit in public, and so on.

Cf. Tamanaha (2006, 63): as is also the case in law, it often only becomes clear how to apply moral norms in an actual situation. See also, *infra*, no. 33. Comparisons of law and ethics are just as rare as studies that investigate a problem from both a legal and an ethical perspective. The lawyer interested in a playful introduction to how ethics deals with dilemmas is referred to the Isabel Dalhousie series of the Scots author and jurist Alexander McCall Smith. Although some may doubt whether norms that are not enforced by the state are followed, these norms can be legally relevant as 'social norms'. See Posner (2000).

Law and ethics are not the only normative disciplines. Economics is also regarded as such, in so far as it aims to say something about how welfare in society is best distributed and about what to do in specific situations. In the last decades, however, this approach (particularly by Rosenberg (1992)) has had to give way to a more empirical perspective from which economic phenomena are only *explained* (usually by way of mathematical models). See Backhouse (1997, 108) and *infra*, no. 57. The normative version of economics has this in common with legal science: there is no one right answer but one can always debate what ought to be. This leads Dow (2002, 3) to ask: 'Is disagreement the sign of an immature science; given time will we all converge on the same answers? Or is there something particular about economics which makes this impossible?' As will become clear in Chapter III, the latter is the only right answer for the legal discipline.

4. LAW AS SPONTANEOUS ORDER

27. Theoretical Background

An approach focusing on what the law ought to be without making itself dependent either on the authoritative institutions (in particular national legislatures and courts), or on what works empirically requires more explanation than has been offered up to this point. This explanation, which pays attention to the *method* of establishing what the law ought to be is offered in Chapter III. In the remainder of this section, I will consider the theoretical framework in which the development of private law is seen as an evolutionary process that has led to a largely spontaneous order (as opposed to a legal order created by the official authorities).

The idea that law can be seen as the product of an evolutionary process is not new in itself: Von Savigny (1831) and Maine (1861) are the best-known proponents of this idea. Remarkably enough, however, this view has disappeared in the last century and has been generally replaced by legal theories that see law as a creation of competent authorities (in brief – legal positivism) or as part of some transcendental nature or culture (in brief – natural law). Particularly in the field of private law, the validity of a rule is often made dependent on the choice of a legislature or court. To look at law as a set of rules that has spontaneously grown under the influence of both external and internal factors largely disappeared as a valid perspective. This is a pity because evolutionary insights sometimes match the law surprisingly well. Furthermore, applying these insights can lead to a restoration of the ties between law and other academic disciplines. See, with many details, Smits (2002b) and Zumbansen & Calliess (2011). Daniel Dennett (1995, 21) was right to identify Darwin's evolutionary theory as 'the single best idea anyone has ever had' and Wilson (1998) even claims that evolutionary theory offers the only explanation for structural change, regardless of the discipline involved (Wilson 1998).

It should be emphasized that an evolutionary explanation is not the only possible way to fill the gap between focusing on the positive law and a non-normative approach. Alternative views are possible, provided they leave space for other sources of law than those that fit in with a positivist approach. To think in terms of Kelsen's 'Grundnorm' or Hart's 'Rule of Recognition' does not meet this requirement: the rise of European norms and of private regulation makes it increasingly difficult to use these criteria to decide upon what is law and what is not. See also Hesselink (2009, 42) and Calliess & Zumbansen (2010).

Despite the many variations in evolutionary thinking, the core of the theory of evolution as developed by Charles Darwin in *On the Origin of Species* (1859) is clear enough. It is that change in organisms takes place through natural selection. The individual members of a species organize their lives so as to produce the most adaptive offspring and in doing so, they necessarily adapt themselves to changing circumstances. The species best able to adapt itself will eventually survive and species failing to adapt will become extinct.

The idea that development is the result of a process of

natural (spontaneous) selection has been applied to many other disciplines outside biology, including the history of science (Popper), political theory (Hayek), ethics (socio-biology), economics and psychology. These last two fields have developed real sub-disciplines of evolutionary economics and psychology with their own extensive literature and professorial chairs. In all of these fields, the thought of an unalterable human nature or a conscious design is abandoned in favour of the idea of natural selection. Thus, the spontaneous development of social and political systems of morality and economics is studied.

> In classic Darwinism, this 'struggle for life' can only occur if certain requirements are met. First, there must be variation in species (otherwise some species could not survive better than others). Secondly, the variation must concern variation in fitness (understood as the ability to survive and reproduce, some species being more able to adapt themselves to changing circumstances than others). Thirdly, the characteristics constituting the fitness of the species must be inherited, meaning that they must be able to be transferred from one generation to the next.

The law can also be seen as the product of a process of natural selection.

> This means that the three Darwinian requirements for natural selection need to be applied to the law. The variation in species then consists of the existence of diverse *national* (and sometimes European) legal rules to solve identical problems. These rules mainly evolved in national (socio-economic and cultural) environments. They relate to essential differences between jurisdictions that reflect differing views of society (such as in levels of solidarity, of duties to help others, levels of social security, and so on).
>
> Secondly, these rules are also likely to vary in fitness. Many of the present day rules in the various European countries are the result of a long evolution during which they were adapted to the environment they had to operate in. According to evolutionary theory, other rules that once existed in these countries must

have been eliminated in this process of natural selection and any change in the environment in the future would – again – lead to the adaptation of present rules. Some rules may become extinct while others become more dominant. Legal history has telling examples of this process. Thus, the rule on *laesio enormis* and the *numerus clausus* of contracts in Roman law had to go because they were no longer fit for the economic environment after the Middle Ages. Rules on animal trials were abolished because of new societal insights and the rule that only men could vote for Parliament had to be replaced because of a changing societal and political environment.

The third requirement for natural selection – that the characteristics constituent of the fitness of the species must be inherited – is more problematic in the context of law. This is due to the simple fact that descendants taking over the genes of their predecessors do not exist. Rules do not procreate in the literal sense of the word. But one can think of an analogy with genes. In evolutionary economics, it was suggested that accepted *routines* played the same role in firms as genes in organisms: routines provide the firm with a *stable identity* that endures over time and – just like genes – programme its behaviour. The same analogy can be used in law. Rules are not just rules: they are learnt by students and applied in practice. Normally, agents (in our case, the legal actors) will not deviate from these rules because of their deference to legal certainty and equality. In this sense, the practice of application is being transferred from one generation to another. And just like genes in biological organisms, these rules may gradually change under the influence of a changing environment (society).

The possibility of applying these general requirements for evolution to the law allows us to see legal change as a process dependent on both nature (the inherent characteristics) and nurture (the environment) in the law. See on all this Smits (2002b).

28. Some Consequences

Several insights follow from this view of law as a spontaneously growing order, in which the various surviving jurisdictions are to be seen as the product of natural selection.

In the first place, law is no longer seen as the product of

conscious *design*, but as the result of a long process of trial and error. This makes the law less suited for conscious decision-making than some would assume. Many rules have acquired a place in the legal system because they have survived the test of time. As David Friedman puts it: 'A system of legal rules is not entirely, perhaps not chiefly, the product of deliberate human design; to a considerable extent it represents the unplanned outcome of a large number of separate decisions, by legislators (. . .) or judges (. . .). It is therefore possible that such a system may have no objective for us to find.'

Friedman (2000, 4). This is of immediate relevance to the debate about European private law: cf. Von Bar & Clive (2009a). The *Study Group on Social Justice in European Private Law* (2004) made an ardent plea for a debate about the desired level of social justice in the European Union before provisions to be included in a European instrument of private law were drafted. The group claimed that because of the one-sided focus that the European Union has on the promotion of the internal market, a 'European' view of justice in contract law would be lacking, unlike the case in national law. This is why a 'social justice agenda' should be developed: 'At the heart of the social justice agenda beats the concern about the distributive effects of the market order. The rules of contract law shape the distribution of wealth and power in modern societies. (. . .) A modern statement of the principles of the private law of contract needs to recognise its increasingly pivotal role in establishing distributive fairness in society' (Study Group 2004, 665). This view connects to Kronman (1980).

In my opinion, this overly emphasizes a vision of Europe as a *makeable* society. The best rules for Europe in my view are not determined by some omnipotent legislature that can change the existing distribution of power and wealth – if this is what one wants to do. Of course the legislature sometimes has to intervene to look after the interests of the weak but this does not mean that this should disrupt the entire relationship between freedom of contract and protection. To me, the law is not primarily the result of conscious choice but rather of spontaneous development. I referred to Hayek (1973–1979 and 1988) in previous work. See, for criticism, Hesselink (2010).

As will be shown below (no. 35), this means that it would be contrary to the nature of private law to consider it as completely subordinate to some political goal: such a view would mean that if the goal were not achieved, private law would have failed. In my view, it is not the state that can decide *ex ante* which purposes private law should serve; at best, the state can correct the result *ex post* (Weinrib 1995, 212). Moreover, a redistribution of wealth through contract law would not work: its most likely effect would be that a party would no longer enter into a contract with a 'weaker' party because it would then run the risk that the contract would not be valid. Fried (1981, 106) framed this point in the following manner: 'Redistribution is not a burden to be borne in a random, ad hoc way by those who happen to cross paths with persons poorer than themselves. Such a conception, heart-warmingly spontaneous though it may be, would in the end undermine our ability to plan and to live our lives as we choose.'

A second consequence of viewing private law from an evolutionary perspective is that it is less subordinate to a process of political and democratic decision-making than is sometimes asserted.

The work on the Draft Common Frame of Reference (DCFR) for European Private Law (Von Bar & Clive 2009a) has brought this matter to the foreground. For many authors, the creation of a European private law is primarily a political process: the right balance between the market and social justice (or autonomy and protection) should be established in a democratic way and should not be left to academics only. To consult practitioners and stakeholders in drafting the DCFR is not enough: the European Parliament and national legislatures should also be involved in order to prevent the DCFR from being *Professorenrecht*. Van Zelst (2008, 244–245) formulates this as follows: 'First of all, the scholars that are involved in the drafting of the DCFR lack democratic legitimacy. The group represents neither all of the populations of the member states, nor their political convictions. Secondly, it is questionable whether professors should be vested with the translation of social-political reality into legislation. In a democratic society, this would seem to principally be the task of the (democratically legitimised) legislature (. . .).'

> This view, clearly inspired by the claim of the *Critical Legal Studies* movement that all law is politics (Kennedy 1976), cannot be accepted. In my view, private law is not just another policy area with which instrumental goals are achieved. It only has to be submitted to democratic decision-making if it is seen as an instrument to achieve a political goal (cf. Tamanaha 2006). This is in conformity with our understanding of private law: it is usually seen as independent of the state and as having its own 'rationality' (Weinrib 1995). Private law developed gradually throughout the ages and reflects the norms desired by the community where these rules evolved. This does not mean that private law is 'neutral' or would not be full of choices made by citizens, legislatures and courts, but it does mean that democratic decision-making is less important than in many other fields. See, with many details, Smits (2009a) and Jansen (2010) for an historical account of how so-called 'non-legislative codifications' (including the *Corpus Iuris Civilis*) have often derived their legitimacy from the fact that they were simply applied in practice.

The view that private law can be seen as a spontaneous (self-developing) order has still a third consequence: it also means that this order provides us with knowledge about what our view of the law ought to be. In the prevailing (positivist) view of the law, legal rules can be changed at any moment depending on what the competent legislature decides to do. However, this view is less suited to a private law that primarily aims to facilitate parties for whom the mere fact that *some* rule exists is more important than the actual contents of this rule.

> In a Darwinian view of law, society is not regulated by norms that are imposed from the outside but, instead, all law is the provisional end result of an everlasting development. It is therefore an historically grown (and still growing) organism. Holmes (1881 [2004]) also saw law as an historically developed collective experience. Cf. MacIntyre (1981, 121ff.) and Jansen (2005, 759).

The final consequence of considering law as an evolutionary system is that it facilitates the explanation of how law is dependent on its internal structure, shaped by past transformations that are now irreversible. This *nature* of the organism is now often considered to be a constraint on change. The path law has taken in the past thus affects its future development. The problem with laws based on this 'path dependent' view is that the result from this evolutionary process often does not produce the best possible solution. In economics, the result may not be the most efficient organizations and in law it may not be the 'best' rules. Thus, alternative categorizations of the sources of obligations are certainly possible, but the persistent use of the distinctions made by Gaius and his successors throughout the ages have set the agenda.

The question whether an old rule will make way for a new one is dependent on the extent to which the legal actors are prepared to deviate from existing practices – that is governed by maximizing principles such as legal certainty, equality and efficiency. If the costs of this change are too high compared to what the changed environment requires, it is not likely that any change will occur. Put differently, the external pressure for a change of law needs to be so high that it exceeds the costs of change. However, under such circumstances, the best solution will not always evolve. Francis Bacon once wrote in *The New Organon* (1620 [1960, 89]): 'In matters of state a change even for the better is distrusted, because it unsettles what is established; these things resting on authority, consent, fame and opinion, not on demonstration.'

See, on Gaius and the use of his *summa divisio* throughout history, Watson (1994). The distinction between obligations arising from contract, delict, or in another manner (and subsequent categorizations based on this) still determines our mode of thinking. Attempts to trade this in for a system that does more justice to reality (such as P.S. Atiyah's proposal to rewrite the law of obligations in terms of benefit and reliance) have had little success. It is inherent in law that it will only slowly move away from well established conceptions, or as Gordon (2007, 366) states: 'Following existing practices may be more likely to gain the necessary approval.' Gordon (2007, 372) refers to Stair's *Institutions of the Law of Scotland* (I.1.15): 'The nations are more happy, whose laws have entered by long custom, wrung out from their debates upon particular cases (. . .). But in statutes the lawgiver must at once balance the conveniences and inconveniences, wherein he may and often doth fall short.' Vranken (2006, 16) is critical of this tethering to the past, stating that in essence it is forcing legal actors only to jump 'with feet of clay'. This is, of course, no hindrance to legal academics in being as creative as possible (cf. *infra*, no. 50).

The extent to which these consequences will in fact occur depends on the field in question. They will be more apparent in private law than in administrative law or tax law. New fields of law often emerge to realize certain policy goals, meaning that a sufficiently developed normative framework does not exist. It makes more sense then to test the rule on the extent to which it achieves this goal than on how it fits in with the system. In other words, if the legal system is more advanced (has its own 'rationality'), it can fulfil the role of an objective and autonomous whole more adequately. This is presumably also why the discipline of private law is often seen as the field best suited to learn 'how to think like a lawyer.'

As will become apparent in Chapter III, law often needs to reconcile contradictory 'goals'. While this goal is clear in medicine (to ensure the health of people), the aim to be achieved in law is much less clear and this means that the arguments are inevitably normative: one can always dispute what one should do or refrain from doing in law. The normative authority that remains is then how a legal rule or decision fits into 'the system': the conflicting interests (for example, deterrence and protection) have already been weighed. Cf. Weinrib (1995) and Friedman (2000, 4).

The more law is treated as an instrument to achieve a certain goal, the less useful it is to regard it as the product of a spontaneous order. It is well known that Von Jhering was one of the first to see the law's aim – contrary to the Historical School – as achieving a goal (*Law as a Means to an End*, (1877)). Since that time, law has no longer been seen as an autonomous and coherent system that can reflect immutable principles. The non-instrumental view of law in the eighteenth and nineteenth century changed into a more instrumental view in the twentieth century. The present emphasis on an economic and empirical analysis of law – and the threat that a normative approach is no longer seen as useful – is the culmination of this. See, with many details, Tamanaha (2006).

29. What is Next? What is Legally Required?

In this chapter, the question of how the law ought to read has been elevated to the core question of legal scholarship. The next step is to ask how this is to be ascertained. In other words, which method should be used to determine what one is legally obliged to do if one cannot have recourse to the authority of democratically legitimated institutions? This question is addressed in the next chapter.

III. Methodology of normative legal science

1. LAW AS THE DISCIPLINE OF CONFLICTING ARGUMENTS

30. Introduction

How does one determine what one is legally obliged to do? It is clear that, in the view of legal scholarship that has been defended above, this question cannot be answered by simply relying on the authority of legislatures and the courts. What then, are the factors relevant to answering this question? This chapter argues that the core of the normative approach is that there is not one answer to what legally ought to be. If the law provides rules for a society and the views on how to regulate this society differ – which is necessarily the case – there must also be different views of what ought to be. The academic-legal method must therefore reflect this important insight. It means that legal science is not about physical reality but about the world of ideas. It is a discipline in which arguments for and against various possible solutions to legal problems are identified and thought through. This makes the legal discipline pre-eminently argumentative.

See, apart from Collier (1991) (mentioned *supra*, no. 23) and Singer (2009), what Rubin (1988, 1893) says about the activity of legal academics: 'The conflict of norms is the essence of normatively-based scholarship (. . .). The entire point of standard legal scholarship is to explore and contrast the pragmatic implications of conflicting normative positions.'

This approach to law has the distinct advantage that the legal discipline is more closely connected to other academic fields in which so-called self-evident knowledge must always be disputed anew. Even if there is consensus about the appropriateness of a legal rule, it must be continuously debated by analysing the arguments for and against it. Law as an academic discipline would have perished long ago if a general consensus on how the law should read ended the debate.

It seems appropriate to cite the English essayist, Matthew Arnold (see Collier 1991, 152): 'That is what I call living by ideas: when one side of a question has long had your earnest support, when all your feelings are engaged, when you hear all round you no language but one, when your party talks this language like a steam-engine and can imagine no other, – still to be able to think, still to be irresistibly carried, if so it be, by the current of thought to the opposite side of the question (. . .).'

The mere fact that one can dispute the desirability of constitutional review or positive discrimination, or even the admissibility of the death penalty, does not make the law less of an academic discipline. This is because the task of legal science does not consist of finding 'the' right rule or outcome to a case, but instead consists of identifying the relevant arguments for and against such rules and outcomes. As the main activity of the practicing lawyer may be to exclude all uncertainty, the mission of the legal academic is to question all seemingly certain outcomes.

Long ago, Hugo Grotius emphasized in *De Jure Belli ac Pacis* (II, 23, 1) that doubt about how the law ought to read is at the core of the legal discipline: 'between what we ought and what we ought not to do, there is a medium but it approaches sometimes nearer to one and sometimes to the other extreme'. And in his *In Praise of Folly* of 1511, Erasmus famously qualified law as the most learned of all disciplines because with each different topic it will 'heap glosses upon glosses, and opinions on the neck of opinions'.

31. Structure of this Chapter

This chapter elaborates on the idea of legal science being the discipline of conflicting arguments. The remainder of this section (nos. 32–37) will address why, in law, discussion about the desired outcome is always possible and why non-legal methods, in particular, that attempt to dismiss uncertainty are doomed. Consensus about the normative is often difficult to reach and therefore should not be endlessly pursued. The second section of this chapter (nos. 38–46) will be devoted to the various views on the role of legal science, and the promotion of one view that should preferably be adopted.

32. Searching for the Stone of Wisdom

Legal science's persistent inclination is to exclude uncertainty over what is the right rule or what is the right outcome of a case. Given this inclination, legal academics often follow the rhetorical strategy of the practising lawyer who has every interest in making it appear as if *his* decision is the only right one, and thus to bar all normative debate about whether this is really the case. This causes legal science often to be directed to finding only one possible answer to the question about what is the right course of action. However, it is justifiable to question this perception that there is only one possible view about what ought to be. This will be investigated on the basis of the methods that lawyers tend to use to base their decisions on: the doctrinal (no. 33); the economic (no. 34); and the empirical (no. 35). Attention is also paid to fundamental rights as these are frequently seen as anchors providing certainty about the right outcome (no. 36).

For what follows I was inspired by, and derive arguments from, the work of Joseph William Singer (2009) and Edward L. Rubin (1988). The law is usually expected to be able to decide disputes in an objective and rational way. And yet – as Singer (2009, 903) clearly points out – the question of 'why' a certain rule has been accepted or an outcome has been reached is often not answered in a satisfactory manner. Why is it that one is allowed to use property in the way one wishes and why is it that parties are bound to their contract? Lawyers not satisfied with a mere reference to the authority of legislature or court, and who are aware that their personal opinion is not enough, tend to find refuge in approaches such as the economic analysis of law. However, lawyers should be able to reason why these two (and other) principles are valid *on legal grounds*: this is where the gap observed above arises between positive law and a non-legal approach (see *supra*, no. 25).

33. What Ought to Be? The Doctrinal Approach

Is it possible to say what, legally, ought to be only by consulting legal doctrines? Students usually learn the law by studying doctrine as laid down in textbooks, whilst practitioners use these same textbooks to establish how legislatures, courts and academic authors judge the questions that they have to deal with on a daily basis. However, it needs little explanation to show that the doctrinal system itself will never lead to one given outcome in a dispute of substance. A jurist's real activity consists of making a choice from among the often contradictory views of what legally ought to be. The doctrinal system fulfils an important role in this regard because it offers insight into existing rules and previously decided cases. The doctrinal system, however, will never provide certainty about *how* to decide.

This meaning of legal doctrine is well captured by the Dutch law professor, Herman Schoordijk (1972, 15), who claims that the system forces the legal actor to 'bring his value judgments, that can never be based completely on the existing legal system, into harmony with judgments previously given in practice or theory.' It is a well-known fact that a decision in a new case can never follow from a rule or a previously decided case because the latter can never determine its own field of application (the cases to which it will be applied in the future). This makes it often unclear which rule is to be applied, or whether there is a previously formulated rule at all. And even if there is no doubt about which rule should be applicable, it will almost always leave space for more than one interpretation. See also Singer (2009, 908), who shows that even if normative consensus can be reached about a certain principle, this will be at such an abstract level that it does not create clarity on how to decide a dispute. If the rule on the other hand does offer sufficient guidance, its contents will necessarily be disputed.

Hence, the core of legal activity does not lie in the drafting or application of norms, but in giving a *judgment* in a normative dispute and therefore in a way of *reasoning*. It can be questioned whether this comes sufficiently to the fore in legal education as most teaching materials often fail to offer alternative ways of reasoning. Rather, the law is usually presented as having only one possible solution. This rather narrow-minded approach could be altered if textbooks, as a start, abandoned their approach of using only one national jurisdiction and adopt a broader focus. For example, rather than limiting their scope to German, or some other, national contract law, students could start with European contract law instead. See also *infra*, nos. 40 and 62.

This confirms that the doctrinal method does not offer any normative certainty since it cannot answer the pertinent question of how the law ought to read (so looking at which rule to apply or how to decide a case of substance) as the arguments *behind* the rule or the case are, in the end, decisive.

The temptation of law has long been to build a coherent and self-referential system that can exist, independent of reality, by making use of the *mos geometricus*. However, this will not lead to certainty in applying the law (a re-definition of the value of a legal system is given, *infra*, no. 45.

34. What Ought to Be? The Role of Law and Economics

Now that the doctrinal approach has been shown not to offer sufficient certainty, the question still remains where one might find more certainty in answering the lingering question of what people and organizations legally ought to do. The present approach, which seems to have gained some popularity, is to consult other disciplines outside the legal arena. This explains the rise of an economic analysis of the law, which aims to offer a more rational perspective. Economic analysis takes a utilitarian view and argues for the implementation of legal rules that generate the most social welfare or benefits. In the clear words of Kaplow and Shavell: 'Legal rules should be selected entirely with respect to their effect on the well being of individuals in society. This position implies that notions of fairness like corrective justice should receive no independent weight in the assessment of legal rules.'

See Kaplow & Shavell (2002, 3) and, for the many applications of economic analysis to different fields of law, Posner (2011). The descriptive variant of the field of Law and Economics was briefly mentioned *supra* (no. 13). In the view of Kaplow & Shavell, the social welfare of society as a whole consists of the aggregate of all individual preferences of citizens. The many variations in the definition of social welfare are not discussed here.

At first glance, the application of this utilitarian criterion seems to offer the guidance needed to ban all uncertainty about what societal actors are legally obliged to do. Each rule is then judged on its impact on the welfare of individuals, taking into consideration the incentives provided for the particular action and its costs and benefits. This has the distinct advantage that all the benefits and disadvantages of the rule are brought back to one common denominator, which is social welfare. This means that one value (such as justice) no longer needs to be balanced against another value (such as efficiency). More importantly, with such an objective measure, one can forgo the difficulty of making a normative decision. Put differently, the question of what people ought to do is then answered by way of one general and non-legal criterion: 'What is it that we as individuals value most?'

Although it seems promising, does economic analysis really live up to its promises and, if so, can it replace the normative approach? There are three reasons why this question must be answered in the negative. In the first place, there is the practical difficulty that tying the preferences of people to a single (quantitative) denominator is not only difficult, but it will still require a normative choice since individual preferences about what monetary value to attach to a particular interest differ greatly.

See Singer (2009, 920) for this 'morally constrained utilitarianism': we cannot escape normative argument. Next to this practical difficulty, there is the more fundamental objection that many values (such as the principle of equality or freedom of contract) are simply unfit to be quantified or, at least, it is very difficult to do so. Ultimately, figures alone cannot replace arguments.

The debate about the meaning of economic analysis for the law is not as recent as it may seem. Economics as an ancillary tool for (in particular) private law emerged around 1850 in Germany under the influence of authors such as H. Dankwardt. The approach even became fashionable in the 1880s thanks to the work of Victor Mataja (1888) and Friedrich Kleinwächter (1883). Their general stance was that the economic approach may be useful in so far as one is dealing with the question of how the law *should* read rather than what the law *is*, but that one should be careful about replacing traditional legal analysis with economic analysis.

Secondly, economic analysis of the law is only interested in people's preferences and not in *why* these preferences exist in the first place. Therefore, it does not sufficiently distinguish between relevant and irrelevant reasons for a certain outcome. In law, it is not only (or even primarily) the result that counts, but it is *the reason why* this result was chosen that matters. To quote an example from Singer, slavery is not wrong because the preferences of those who oppose it outweigh the preferences of those who favour it. If this argument were accepted, the dignity of a few could be subordinated to the power of the majority.

Singer (2009, 918). In the legal field, arguing in terms of costs and benefits alone will be ineffective. Otherwise, a party could claim victory simply because its interest or welfare outweighed the interests of the other party or the community's welfare. This cannot be the basis of a convincing legal analysis.

The theory of 'efficient breach' clearly shows the limited value of economic analysis for the normative question about the 'ought'. According to the doctrine of efficient breach, a contracting party may refuse to perform a contract and pay damages instead if this is economically more efficient. A party can thus decide not to perform, if it will be better off without the other party being worse off as a result (because the latter will receive the expectation interest). The premise is that the performances of both parties can be expressed in monetary terms. However, Singer (2009, 945) convincingly shows that this is often not the case. If the party in breach of contract is, for example, a tenant who, before the end of the lease of an apartment for one year, wanted to move somewhere else because he had found a job in another town, it would be efficient if the landlord allowed the tenant to sublet the apartment to a third party – even if this were not allowed in the contract. This seems to lead to an increase in the total amount of welfare: the landlord will still receive the rent, the tenant can take the job without extra costs, and his new employer is also happy because his prospective employee can start on time. However, it is entirely feasible that the landlord may have a non-economic interest in not allowing the subtenant to move. It may be that he has an interest in being paid by this specific tenant. It may also be that he does not want the hassle of looking for a new tenant within the agreed period. Perhaps these interests of the landlord are not relevant but the point is that one needs a *legal* approach to decide upon this. Singer's example shows that the true (normative) question is whether these are legally justified interests of the landlord. This is a question that economic analysis is unable to answer.

The final reason why an economic analysis of the law cannot replace a normative approach is that it assumes from the very beginning a premise that is not universally accepted. It presumes not only that more social welfare is a good thing, but also that each individual is free to determine his or her own preferences. This is a liberal view that will not be shared by everyone: many will say that part of this individual autonomy must *a priori* be given up in order to achieve some degree of social justice for everyone in society.

See Singer (2009, 916). In addition, it should be mentioned that economics also derives its foundations from elsewhere and is at times even dependent on the law itself. Economics presupposes an institutional framework within which, for example, property rights exist that can be freely transferred by way of a contract: the legal *status quo* is as much the starting point in *describing* and *explaining* reality as it is in judging why it should *change* (in the variant of the field of normative Law and Economics).

These limitations do not mean that economic analysis is not useful. As a matter of fact, legal rules are often deliberately designed to achieve pre-set economic goals. Even if this is not the case, it is useful to know about the costs and benefits of implementing a certain rule or reaching a certain judicial decision. However, it is important to distinguish the usefulness of economic analysis in those specific circumstances from its usefulness in answering the question about the 'ought'. Although economic analysis of the law can be a useful tool in answering some legal questions, in the end it is an inadequate tool in answering the question of what laws we ought to follow.

An example of how economic knowledge can feed legal judgments concerns the scope of art. 114 of the Treaty on the Functioning of the European Union (TFEU). This provision provides that the European legislator can adopt measures for the approximation of national provisions tasked with the establishment and functioning of the internal market. However, this is not a general competence to regulate anything related to the internal market of the EU. The European Court of Justice made it clear that a directive or a regulation based on art. 114 must genuinely have as its objective the improvement of the conditions for the establishment and functioning of the internal market. A mere finding of disparities between national rules and of the abstract risk of obstacles to this market is not sufficient to justify a harmonizing measure (CoJ EU 5 October 2000, C-376/98 (concerning tobacco advertising)). This implies that economic research is needed in order to create a *legal* basis for a new European measure aiming to better facilitate the internal market. See Low (2010) for an extensive discussion of what this may lead to.

35. What Ought to Be? The Empirical Approach

The use of empirical research is yet another approach often offered as a helpful tool in determining how the law should read. Particularly in the United States, this has led to an influential view of the law that is usually referred to as 'Pragmatism'. According to Richard Posner, this is an approach that is 'more empirical, more realistic, more attuned to the real needs of real people'.

Posner (1995, 19). A similar concern was voiced by the Dutch author Maurits Barendrecht (2003), who argued that private law may not sufficiently reflect the 'interests, the real preferences of people'. Naturally, one can always debate what the *real* interests of people are.

If law is seen as an instrument to achieve a previously set aim, empirical research is inevitable in determining whether this goal has really been achieved and whether the chosen approach has worked. However, one should not overestimate the importance of empirical research (see also *supra*, no. 16). There are three reasons why this approach cannot be the decisive factor.

First, not all law is instrumental. In the prevailing view, the law still has its own rationality and its success is not dependent on the extent to which it can realize a political goal or serve as an instrument. A different view would not be very democratic since one of the main functions of law is to offer a counterweight to the majority that is setting the goal to be achieved. To claim that the law serves an external goal makes the law itself completely dependent on the desires of the majority. This would characterize the law as a non-normative discipline.

An illustration of how 'law as a means to an end' can form a threat to the rule of law see Tamanaha (2006) and cf. Watson (2006, 212–213). In particular, Weinrib (1995, 6) explains why it would be wrong to see law only as an instrument: 'Because the functionalist goals are justifiable independently and the law's purpose is to reflect them, the study of the law becomes parasitic on the study of the non-legal disciplines (economics, political theory, and moral philosophy) (. . .) that might validate these goals. (. . .) Law provides only the authoritative form into which the conclusions of non-legal thinking are translated. The governing presupposition is that the content of law cannot be comprehended in and of itself, simply as law.' The functionalist is trapped in his view that the law only *serves*, while in reality it also *determines* reality as the conceptual apparatus of the law creates its own reality. See also Feinman (1989, 663), quoted *supra*, no. 9.

Once again, this does not mean that empirical work is not useful. On the contrary, if a rule aims to achieve a certain aim (promote road safety, protect the weaker party, or avoid crime), there is every reason to establish the extent to which this rule is able to succeed in its task. However, one should not make this the only decisive criterion with which to measure success: empirical evidence cannot be decisive in a normative approach. This leads me to two other objections.

First, the results of empirical research only rarely point in one direction. Even if a theme is very well researched, such as the famous question about the deterrent effect of capital punishment, views remain divided about what the empirical evidence actually proves.

This debate received new impetus after Cass Sunstein and Adrian Vermeule showed, on the basis of recent empirical materials, that carrying out the death penalty can have a significant deterrent effect on prospective criminals. In their view, each execution would deter some eighteen murders. On the basis of this 'life-life trade-off' there would no longer be a moral argument against the death penalty: banning execution is equivalent to condemning as yet unidentified innocent people to a premature and violent death. The government, as a *moral agent*, must then look after the interests of these innocent people. The arguments that errors can be made in convicting people and that an execution is irreversible are not convincing enough: 'a legal regime with capital punishment predictably produces far *fewer* arbitrary and irreversible deaths than a regime without capital punishment' (Sunstein & Vermeule 2006, 731). The reliability of the empirical materials was subsequently disputed by, among others, Donohue and Wolfers (2006). After the US Supreme Court had extensively cited Sunstein & Vermeule in *Baze* v. *Rees* (553 U.S. 35 (2008)) – in which carrying out the death penalty by injection was not held to be a violation of the Constitution – even Sunstein retreated from the evidence he had previously characterized as 'powerful' and 'impressive'. Sunstein and Wolfers (2008) subsequently claimed that 'the best reading of the accumulated data is that they do not establish a deterrent effect of the death penalty'.

Another well-researched topic concerns the question of whether a ban on tobacco advertising leads to a fall in the number of smokers. Here too, the answer is not clear. Schneider et al. (1981) show that an advertising ban may help reduce tobacco consumption among young people, but also conclude that adult smokers are not significantly affected by it. Others dispute this seemingly clear conclusion: see the overview by Saffer & Chaloupka (2000). Also, the claim that *common law* jurisdictions are more conducive to economic development than *civil law* jurisdictions will probably remain disputed in perpetuity. The latest development in this subject is the conflict between the empirical materials provided by Shleifer & Glaeser (2002) and the data of others that points in a different direction (cf. Faure & Smits 2011).

The final point is that, although empiricists often claim that they can provide lawyers with objective (non-normative) knowledge, a closer inspection of their claims reveals that this is not really the case. Both the question of what is actually the problem and what is its solution require a normative evaluation. In the end, even the empirical method cannot avoid entanglement with the normative.

This is apparent from the view often held by pragmatists that the law does not primarily reflect the intention of the legislature nor should it be seen as a doctrinal system, but instead it serves to solve a 'real' problem. However, this is not the traditional task of the lawyer: it is not social reality that is the object of his study, but – in the wording of Geoffrey Samuel (2009, 26) – the virtual reality of the legal system, in which the objects derive their value only from their place within this system. This does not mean that lawyers cannot tackle this problem-solving task, but one must be cognizant that, under that scenario, the distinction between a lawyer and a social worker starts to blur. Under the pragmatic ('what works?') approach to law, differences of opinion about the nature of the problem, its importance, and possible solutions will persist. Regarding this last aspect (the solution to the problem), the stone of wisdom is sometimes sought in a *procedure* instead of in a particular substantive rule. This can be at an abstract level (as in John Rawls' *A Theory of Justice* (1999), which attempts to avoid normative conflicts of opinion by starting from a hypothetical process of decision-making), but also at the level of an actual dispute by creating a 'neutral' procedure of conflict resolution. In both cases a problem remains: the abstract level leaves open what should be the outcome in a dispute while, at the substantive level, the adequacy of the procedure can be questioned. Singer (2009, 907) states: 'The unavoidable fact is that no matter how hard we try to define impartial decision procedures, we face persistent disagreement both about basic notions of what is good and right and just and about which procedures are suitably impartial.'

36. What Ought to Be? Fundamental Rights as Cornerstones

The final method of establishing what ought to be in law that is discussed here consists of references to fundamental rights. It is often asserted that it may be true that one can doubt the appropriateness of 'normal' rules or their application but fundamental rights are cornerstones for deciding what people ought to do. For example, one could argue that there is no need to debate the value of the principle of equality and freedom of speech. This argument, however, is not entirely true. First, one only needs to skim any newspaper to see how much debate there is over what freedom of speech actually means. The conflagration spreading across Europe over what it means to 'insult' Muslims is a clear example of this. Secondly, even if consensus exists about the exact contents of a fundamental right, this right will, in an actual dispute, almost always conflict with another fundamental right. Finally, even the basic acceptance of some fundamental rights is debated, in particular with regard to religious orthodoxies.

Cf. Singer (2009, 922): in so far as fundamental rights are undisputed, they are not sufficiently well defined to decide specific cases. Singer's point is confirmed by the debate in Europe about the extent to which fundamental rights can offer guidance in deciding cases between private parties. Although it was claimed that they can have a harmonizing effect (Mak 2007), this is in practice not so evident. In particular, human dignity is a problematic 'universal' right: case law shows that there is much doubt about what it actually requires. In the 'wrongful birth' cases, as decided by different national courts, references are often made to human dignity or some similar concepts but only to support conflicting views. Some of the highest courts in Europe have referred to the general personality right of the child (and the child's dignity) in addressing the question of whether the parents can claim damages from a doctor for the rearing of the child in cases where a doctor's malpractice (a failed vasectomy or other contraceptive treatment) led to an unwanted pregnancy. However, this did not lead to a single uniform outcome: different senates of the German *Bundesverfassungsgericht* (BVerfGE 96, 375 and 88, 203) are divided and the Dutch *Hoge Raad* allows compensation (NJ 1999, 145). the British House of Lords held in *MacFarlane and Another* v. *Tayside Health Board* ([1999] 4 All ER 963) through Lord Steyn: 'Relying on principles of distributive justice I am persuaded that our tort law does not permit parents of a healthy unwanted child to claim the cost of bringing up the child from a health authority or a doctor'. Whether the personality right of the child or the autonomy of the parents should prevail is therefore disputed (see also Lord Millet in *Darlington Memorial Hospital* v. *Rees*, [2004] 1 AC 309 for an emphasis on the autonomy of the parents).

European and international case law also shows how a concept like human dignity lends itself to many different interpretations. In the *Omega*-case (C-36/02, [2004] ECR I-09609), the European Court of Justice explicitly refused to give one European interpretation of what human dignity entails. In the famous *Wackenheim* case, the United Nations Human Rights Committee concluded that the French authorities were allowed to ban 'dwarf tossing' on the grounds of protecting the human dignity of someone who, being 1.14 m. tall, made it his profession to be thrown onto an airbed by clients of a discotheque (*Wackenheim/France*, U.N. Doc. CCPR/C/75/D /854/1999). However, one can also argue for the opposite result by claiming that human dignity does not mean protection of the supposedly weaker party but should be recognized through the autonomy of a contracting party who wants to earn a living by freely choosing this line of work. See Kant (1785[2002, 436]): 'Autonomy is therefore the ground of the dignity of human nature and of every rational nature'. See also, with more details, Smits (2008a).

This also means that reasoning in terms of fundamental rights is an inherently normative activity: undisputed rights do not exist and, in so far as they are generally recognized, they are so indeterminate that they offer only little guidance in deciding a dispute.

The discussion about fundamental rights often takes place in terms of conflicts between rights: if one party invokes a fundamental right, the other party is often able to invoke another one, prompting the need to balance them both. In the famous German suretyship case (BVerfG 19 October 1993, *NJW* 1994, 36), the 21-year-old daughter of a businessman agreed to stand surety for an amount of more than 100 000 DM (approximately €51 000) for her father's debt to a bank. She did so by signing a pre-printed form at the request of a bank employee, who told her: 'Would you just sign here, please? You are not entering into any important obligation: I need this for my files'. The daughter was not very well-educated, was unemployed most of the time, and when she did work (usually in a Hamburg fish factory) she earned an income of only 1150 DM (approximately €590) per month. When her father was no longer able to pay his debts, the bank turned to his daughter. The German Federal Supreme Court held her bound to the contract, reasoning that any adult person knows that signing a contract of suretyship entails a certain risk. The consequence of its judgment was that she not only had to pay 100 000 DM, but also a high monthly interest of 708 DM. In order to meet the monthly subsistence level, she had to earn at least 1800 DM, an income she had never had in her life and was unlikely to receive in the future. This would have been the end of the matter if the daughter had not appealed to the German Constitutional Court, claiming that her fundamental right to private autonomy (art. 2 of the German Constitution), in conjunction with her human dignity, was violated by the civil court. Against this claim based on her dignity, the bank (unsuccessfully) invoked another fundamental right: the freedom of contract that it had exercised that compelled the daughter to honour her contract. This illustrates very well that, in a conflict among private parties, both sides can often invoke a right that is seen as fundamental. The question of which right ought to prevail requires a normative decision.

37. Intermediate Conclusion: Normative Uncertainty is Both Inevitable and Desirable

The clear conclusion to be drawn from the sections above is that it seems impossible to give one uniform answer to what one legally ought to do. Not only does the traditional doctrinal approach fail to give any definitive answers in the abstract or in deciding an actual case, but neither does reasoning on the basis of fundamental rights or making use of non-legal methods lead to any definitive answers.

This does not mean that these approaches are not useful (and this is not disputed at all for the other types of legal science distinguished *supra*, no. 5): they can even be of great service to the normative approach. But it does mean that we need to re-think, for each case, how *precisely* these insights can be beneficial in the field of law. See also Samuel (2008, 314).

If this conclusion is accepted, we can identify two different courses that are open. One way would consist of a continued search for a method that could put an end to normative uncertainty. However, I propose a different way. I am convinced that the core of the legal approach is to *recognize* existing uncertainty: the law can be reduced to disputes about what legally ought to be. This means that we should not try to eliminate normative uncertainty, but should take it as the *starting point* of legal scholarship: if consensus about the normative cannot be reached, we should not strive for it. This means that it is not only *inevitable* that one can dispute the right outcome, it is also *desirable*. Contrary to what is advertised in the

American Declaration of Independence, 'self-evident' truths do not exist in reality.

> Put more bluntly, a claim that suggests any of the methods reviewed here is capable of delivering definitive results is a ruse at best. This view fits in with a longstanding tradition. Aristotle (340 BC [1934, 7]), Grotius and Erasmus (both referred to *supra*, no. 30) all agreed that morality and law cannot offer mathematical certainty and therefore the *nature* of the law as an academic discipline stands in the way of reaching consensus. Cf. Singer (2009, 911): 'normative argument is inescapable' and Rubin (1988, 1853), who makes references to the 'irreducible normativity' of law. This need for permanent debate is therefore the only right point of departure.

Now that (normative) legal scholarship has been defined as a discipline of conflicting arguments, we will explore the consequences of this view in the next section.

2. TOWARDS AN EMPIRICAL-NORMATIVE APPROACH

38. Are Personal Preferences Decisive?

The argument up to this point can easily be summarized. It consists of two consecutive steps. In step one, the question of what people and organizations are legally obliged to do was identified as the core question of legal science. It was also made clear why this question cannot be answered by relying on the authority of institutions, such as legislatures and courts. In step two, the lack of uniformity in answering the question of what one legally ought to do was explained: law is a pre-eminently argumentative discipline. It is now time to take a third step: what does this view mean for the methodology of normative legal science?

It should be noted, first, that within normative legal science, law has not become a matter of personal (political) views, although some would disagree with this assertion. Both Ed Rubin and Martijn Hesselink state that this should be the case, based on the presumption that individuals have different views about the right values in society and that, accordingly, the academic method must also consist in making explicit one's own (for example liberal or social-democrat) normative presuppositions. Or, in other words, whether a certain legal argument can be accepted depends on one's view of what is an ideal society.

> See Rubin (1988, 1893) and Hesselink (2009, 35). The latter argues that each legal academic should therefore indicate on his website, or in the publication itself, his political preferences. Only after a transparent disclosure of these preferences can one truly determine whether someone's views about the law are consistent.
>
> Another reaction to the idea that what one legally ought to do is inherently uncertain, is to emphasize the importance of rhetoric in legal discourse. Law does not then find its foundation in some objective criterion, but in convincing others of the rightness of one's own arguments. Thus, Chaïm Perelman (1980, 129) claims that legal reasoning is nothing more than 'an argumentation aiming to persuade and convince those whom it addresses, that such a choice, decision or attitude is preferable to concurrent choices, decisions and attitudes'. However, a problem with this view is that the question whether an argument is convincing for the other party, or for the forum or public at large, cannot be answered without consulting existing law: the successful orator will always have to give substantive reasons that matter to the law. This being the case, rhetoric will have to rest on a firmer foundation than just the power of persuasion.

In my view, this approach to what people ought to do in law is too dependent on the political views of an individual. The consequence of this would be that any sensible debate about what is the right view is, in the end, no longer possible. A proponent, for example, of more social justice in the law can simply tell others that their view is just an opinion, as much as his, without any need to persuade the other. This would end all discussion.

See also Singer (2009, 902): the choice for a particular solution is then no longer determined by a rational balancing of arguments, but has become a matter of faith. Moreover, an overall political view will – again – only seldom lead to guidelines on how to decide actual cases.

39. The Empirical-Normative Method

My point of departure is therefore elsewhere. Even though one can always debate what people legally ought to do, guidance can be derived from existing normative frameworks. The type of guidance that I am advocating, however, is different from the usual kind. Existing law is mostly studied as a whole body of authoritative statements made by institutions. This system is usually consulted in order to establish how the positive law reads – a method that was set aside before and labelled as insufficiently academic. What is therefore needed is a shift in perspective: existing jurisdictions should be considered as providing empirical material on how to deal with conflicting arguments. The academic method then consists of bringing these arguments into the open and discussing the consequences of choosing one argument over others. In this new perspective, case law and legislation are no longer authoritative statements about what is law within a certain jurisdiction but, rather, a source of information about the power of a particular normative argument.

This means that the law is no longer studied as a system of binding decisions (flowing from the formal sources of law) or as a functional system (emphasising the extent to which law realizes an external goal), but as a *normative* system where arguments can be put forward in favour of and against certain outcomes. This is a way to act upon the call made by Singer (2009, 931) to develop 'structures of normative reasoning that recognize the inevitability both of controversial normative premises and procedures (. . .)' with the added benefit of allowing us to learn from experiences elsewhere.

This method can be defined as the empirical-normative method. Under this approach, existing jurisdictions are treated as laboratories for dealing with conflicting normative positions. They show which arguments exist in favour of, and against, any particular solution, which arguments have prevailed elsewhere and how the result has been received in that jurisdiction. These insights can be made accessible for one's own jurisdiction through comparison.

This method combines the benefits of the normative approach (that is, what ought to be is a matter of which argument carries most weight) with those of an empirical approach (that is, by considering how this argument functions elsewhere and how it could function in one's own jurisdiction). Other than for the strictly empirical approach discussed earlier (no. 16), this has the advantage that empirical insights will already have been translated into the legal context. The insight into how arguments function may also be derived from one's own jurisdiction but in my view this is an approach that is too thin (see *infra*). The ultimate goal of legal scholarship is to explore conflicting normative positions and the best way to do this is by comparing situations in different jurisdictions. See also Rubin (1988, 1893) and Schoordijk (1972), who emphasizes that the task of the jurist is to explore all possible cases.

The metaphor of jurisdictions as laboratories can be traced back to the famous statement of Louis Brandeis in *New State Ice Co.* v. *Liebmann* (285 U.S. 262 (1932)): 'To stay experimentation in things social and economic is a grave responsibility. Denial of the right to experiment may be fraught with serious consequences to the Nation. It is one of the happy incidents of the federal system that a single courageous State may, if its citizens choose, serve as a laboratory; and try novel social and economic experiments without risk to the rest of the country.'

The empirical-normative method needs to make use of materials from different jurisdictions: to consider only one's own law is too meagre an academic approach to law. Comparison with other jurisdictions, and even with other normative systems (such as ethics and social norms), shows how solutions adopted elsewhere function. This may mean that the factual situation elsewhere – the realization that some rule fulfils a useful function – can lead to the normative judgment that this should also be accepted as the right one for one's own jurisdiction.

Present-day comparative law is primarily aimed at a comparison of national jurisdictions. Glenn (2003, 844) rightly points out that normative judgements should not exclusively be found in the law of states. Instead, a 'method of normative reasoning, within and across state law' must be developed. In the famous English case of *McFarlane* v. *Tayside Health Board* (2000 SC (HL) 15), Lord Steyn held: 'The discipline of comparative law does not aim at a poll of solutions adopted in different countries. It has the different and inestimable value of sharpening our focus on the weight of competing considerations'. This well reflects what legal comparison is about: it is by comparing that one realizes that an acceptance of a different argument can lead to better outcomes. One does not need a *tertium comparationis* (see *supra*, no. 15) for this: the mere fact that cases are not *completely* comparable is not a barrier to learning from elsewhere. See on incommensurability also *infra*, no. 46.

In an increasing number of cases, courts refer to foreign laws to establish the value of particular arguments. A well-known American example concerns the constitutionality of the death penalty for crimes committed by 16- and 17-year olds. The United States Supreme Court found support for its view that execution is not permitted in these cases, basing its argument in part on the fact that 'the overwhelming weight of international opinion' is against the death penalty for juveniles. An argument cannot be derived only from how a rule is perceived elsewhere, but it is possible to look at other jurisdictions to consider the *effect* of a rule. When debating the question of the legal drinking age, inspiration can be drawn from jurisdictions where this age is 16 (Italy), 18 (Spain), 20 (Japan) or 21 (United States) years, or completely absent (Albania), and the effects of these differences can be established.

See *Roper* v. *Simmons* (543 U.S. 551 (2005)). See also Justice Breyer's dissent in *Printz* v. *United States* (521 U.S. 898, at 977 (1997)): 'we are interpreting our own Constitution, not those of other nations, and there may be relevant political and structural differences between their systems and our own. But their experience may nonetheless cast an empirical light on the consequences of different solutions to a common legal problem.' Markesinis & Fedtke (2005, 97–98) and Dannemann (2006, 396) also point to this empirical use of foreign law: comparison can show the consequences of rules and how they should be evaluated. As an example, Dannemann (2006, 398) mentions the newly established rule in Germany that no longer requires all family members (husband, wife and their common children) to have the same surname. Before this change, it was feared that it could lead to tensions within the family. But, in Latin America there is no uniformity of surnames within the family and this does not mean that family ties are any weaker. Another example concerns the right to cure malperformance of a contract as it exists under German law (see *infra*, no. 42). Acceptance of such a right does not necessarily make the law of contractual remedies more difficult to deal with, as the Dutch legislature once feared.

There is, however, an important difference between a court's reasoning and legal scholarship. While the court (or legislator) will eventually have to make a choice and one argument will prevail over the others, legal scholarship can confine itself to sketching alternative approaches and thinking through the relevant arguments. Legal academics can thus greatly contribute to the making of a better decision but they cannot control whether practice will make use of the insights they provide: this is a matter for the institutions. In other words, while legal science casts doubt, legal practice aims to end all uncertainty.

Legislators and courts have themselves been inspired by foreign laws because they are interested in the arguments used by their counterparts elsewhere. Whether liability for pure economic loss should exist is not dependent on the question of whether English or French law allow this, but on the substantive arguments that plead in favour of or against this solution and that may have been discussed in an illuminating way in a foreign decision, a legislative memorandum, or even a textbook. Eventually, however,

> the national legislator or court will need to decide for itself what it considers to be the best outcome for its own jurisdiction. The legitimacy of such a comparative inspiration is almost undisputed in Europe. It is even seen as counterproductive not to profit from insights obtained elsewhere (even though this may not happen as frequently as one would wish). The basis of this view is that no one jurisdiction is unique.
>
> As popular as this view is in Europe, its value is heavily debated (at least so far as the judiciary is concerned) in the United States. The reason for this is best explained by US Supreme Court Justice Antonin Scalia (1996), who wrote: 'We judges of the American democracies are servants of our peoples, sworn to apply (. . .) the laws that those peoples deem appropriate. We are not some international priesthood empowered to impose upon our free and independent citizens supra-national values that contradict their own.' The American Constitution, in particular, is a unique expression of the nation and the task of the judge is to help form this nation by respecting the Constitution. When the United States Supreme Court in *Roper* v. *Simmons* (see *supra*) referred to the international consensus, Scalia heavily criticized this: 'I do not believe that the meaning of (. . .) our Constitution should be determined by the subjective views of five Members of this Court and like-minded foreigners (. . .).'

As well as adopting ideas from foreign arguments, legal scholars can also investigate the adaptability of these arguments within their own jurisdiction: one argument may be better than another because it fits better with the existing normative framework. The question of whether the doctrine of *leasio enormis* should be accepted, or to what extent the consumer needs to be protected against a professional party, can thus also be answered *within* a certain jurisdiction.

The remainder of this chapter will elaborate on this particular method. Attention will first (no. 40) be paid to the need for a new type of (normative) scholarship that is devoted to the identification of arguments. This is not only important to the study of national law, but also for newly established international fields such as European private law or European criminal law. The age-old method of formulating and applying rules no longer seems fit for this field (no. 41). Next, the extent to which legal scholarship must search for universal principles is considered (no. 42), a question also relevant to deciding when we can speak of legal uniformity (no. 43). Finally, the proposed approach calls into question how to decide a dispute and what is the role of doctrine in doing so (nos. 44–46).

40. An Argumentative Discipline

In the last two centuries, legal science has largely focused on formulating rules and creating doctrinal systems. Not only did the legislature draft rules through, for example, comprehensive codifications of private and criminal law, legal science played the role of a critical follower of the authoritative institutions.

This emphasis on the importance of rules and of the legal system is understandable from the internal perspective of legal scholarship, which has been noted previously. From this perspective, there is little need to criticize the importance of the system of rules for reaching a decision in an actual case. Even if the outcome in a case does not automatically follow from the legal system, this is not a problem in a relatively homogeneous national society: if there is one prevailing legal culture ('morality'), the main actors in the legal community will know how to reach a reasonable outcome.

> Put differently, even if a rule does not determine its own field of application (see *supra*, no. 33), one does not have to reflect fundamentally upon how a decision is to be taken: what the legal system means in an actual case is determined by its 'internal morality' (Fuller, 1969, 33). This reflects the prevailing opinion of what is right. Even without relevant rules, one would probably come to a result that is generally accepted.

There are two reasons why this view no longer reflects the present situation adequately. First, there is no longer one prevailing morality at the national level. Views on the right thing to do differ between groups on many issues. This calls for a greater emphasis on the process of argumentation and on the question of why a certain outcome is reached. Reference to the existing legal system becomes less and less adequate. This means that legal science should be less focused on rules, the construction of the legal system, or finding the 'right' outcome, and more on the relevant arguments, and the way in which a conflict between these arguments must be solved.

> The less uniform the set of values a society has, the more substantive reasoning it needs. The text and its interpretation are then less important and one continuously needs to give reasons in favour of, or against, a particular outcome. Atiyah (1980, 1255) describes this development away from rules towards doing justice in the circumstances of the case as 'a profound shift away from principles to pragmatism'.

Secondly, increasing Europeanization also leads to a legal science that is less focused on rules and systems and more on substantive reasoning. Except in so far as some very general principles, such as freedom of contract and protection of property, are concerned, a uniform European morality does not exist: even if uniform rules can be identified, they will be interpreted differently in various jurisdictions. This means that the emphasis should no longer be on the formulation and application of rules, but on the substantive arguments behind them. The German sociologist Ulrich Beck rightly claims that law, and the way in which we describe it, must be re-thought in the light of an increasing internationalization.

> In the grandiloquent jargon of Beck (2003, 458), increasing 'denationalisation' and 'transnationalisation' should lead us to a 'reconceptualisation' of law within a new cosmopolitan framework in order to avoid the legal discipline becoming 'a museum of antiquated ideas'. In the nation-state, law consists of rules that have come into being on the authority of the relevant institutions and which – if need be with the help of state power – can be enforced by a democratically elected government (Morgan & Yeung 2007, 303–304). The way in which law is usually described is in conformity with this: to describe law by way of rules suggests

that these rules can be relatively easily applied, thus offering the necessary legal certainty and equality. Our understanding of the law is in this respect, largely determined by what rules can *do* at the national level (Twining & Miers 2010). A law that is not based on this process of national democratic decision-making should therefore preferably be described in another way, rather than through clear-cut rules.

41. Example: the Draft Common Frame of Reference for European Private Law

This plea that legal science should be turned into an argumentative discipline can be substantiated by reference to the recently published Draft Common Frame of Reference for European Private Law (DCFR). This document gives too little account of the function it has.

The DCFR (Von Bar & Clive 2009a) aims to define principles, definitions and model rules for a European private law. It consists of detailed rules divided over ten 'books' and covers both the law of obligations and parts of property law. The DCFR is presented as an 'academic' text: it may be that the European legislature can make use of it in revising the existing *acquis*, but it has an autonomous role in teaching and research and in being a source of inspiration for national legislatures and courts.

I am of the opinion that the DCFR suffers from so-called 'methodological nationalism' (a term coined by the sociologist Herminio Martins; see Smits 2010): in drafting rules aimed to be used primarily as a non-binding source of inspiration, the drafters' underlying presuppositions were based on the role of law in the nation-state. Our traditional way of thinking, as developed for law within a national society, is then transplanted to the European level. The DCFR is an example of drafting and structuring rules similar to a national code. There are three reasons why this can be qualified as methodological nationalism.

First, we should recognize that private law at the European level will continue to flow from various sources: there will be a continuous infusion of private law emanating not only from national and European sources, but also from private regulation.

This multi-layered structure of European private law prompts the question, at which regulatory level are these issues best regulated? The entire private law system can, in any event, no longer be governed by only one piece of legislation as this would be contrary to the allocation of normative powers between the member states and the European Union. The DCFR, however, seems to shows little evidence of this insight that private law is a multi-layered system (cf. *supra*, no. 17) since it aims to cover the whole of the law of obligations and other parts of private law as if it were a national code.

A second feature of national codifications is that there is usually little doubt about what the relevant rules should be and who should choose them. This is because, at the national level, there usually is a generally accepted criterion to decide which rules are to be incorporated in the code and because there is a generally accepted procedure to adopt such rules (in most cases a national democratic decision process). At the European level, such consensus is lacking. This makes it all the more important to make use of a clear method when deciding which rules should be part of the DCFR and who should adopt the final text. According to the drafters of the DCFR, its provisions are based on a comparative analysis of the law of the member states and the applicable European law. But this method is not very convincing if one does not know how this comparative method was applied: did the drafters look for the common denominator of the relevant jurisdictions, or for the solution considered to be the 'better' one and, if so, for what reason? Discussion about the contents of the provisions is difficult if the drafters do not explain the motivations behind their choice.

The final issue is whether the function of the DCFR has anything to say about the way in which rules should be formulated. In the nation-state, laws usually appear to consist of authoritative rules backed by a coercive force that is exercised by legitimately constituted democratic institutions. The way in which laws are often represented matches these characteristics: describing the law by way of rules implies that these rules can create the legal certainty and equality needed to guide those affected by them. In this sense, our understanding of rules is closely related to what these rules can *do* at the national level: they organize society, presuming that the rules came into being in a democratic process and can therefore be enforced by the state institutions. It is thus the national democratic process that enables policy trade-offs to be made transparently and authoritatively. The question is whether law beyond the national state should be represented in the same way, in particular when – as is the case with the DCFR – the aim of the provisions is not to influence the conduct of private parties directly and be enforced, but to be primarily a source of inspiration. The answer must be in the negative: in my view, the functions of legal texts are largely dependent on how they are presented. Thus, a national civil code needs to be presented in a different way from a set of rules that should help to improve the existing *acquis*, should inspire legislators and courts across Europe or play a role in legal science and teaching. The rules are presently drafted as if they could be applied in the real world, but this is not the case (see *supra*, no. 40). My view is that they should reflect the competing principles that exist and how, despite differences in *outcome* in actual disputes, similar *arguments* play a role in making choices among these principles. With this in mind, a more discursive text, sketching alternatives, is to be preferred. See also, with more details, Smits (2010).

42. Legal Science Not About Finding Universal Principles

The view expressed above also has implications for whether legal science should search for universal principles. In the course of history, there has been a constant desire to find principles that are as certain as those in the natural sciences amongst the amorphous mass of rules and cases that inundate the legal field. However, as soon as the central question of legal scholarship is about what people should do as a matter of law, the value of drafting principles is limited: any lawyer knows that, when a case has to be decided, legitimate principles will always contradict each other in the end.

See, on the universal pretentions of legal science, also *infra*, no. 8. The recent phenomenon of academics looking for the principles of European private law (such as the PECL, the Principles of European Tort Law and the DCFR) is a distant echo of the universalism practised by comparative lawyers in the early twentieth century. Around that time, Raymond Saleilles, Edouard Lambert and others aimed to uncover the common institutions and principles to end what they considered to be only coincidental differences among jurisdictions.

Instead of drafting uniform rules or principles, the emphasis should be on exposing the various arguments for and against particular solutions, and on exposing how these arguments work in different jurisdictions. Competition between arguments leads to progress because one can learn from experiences elsewhere.

See, on the importance of competition over legal rules (or arguments or ideas) and the learning processes this generates, for example, Wilhelmsson (2002) and Smits (2002b). This is also the reason why I do not believe that the Draft Common Frame of Reference for European Private Law shows 'how much national private laws resemble one another and have provided mutual stimulus for development and indeed how much those laws may be regarded as regional manifestations of an overall common European legacy' (Von Bar 2009b, 6). I am also convinced that, in the field of private law, the European member states have a lot in common (see *infra*, no. 43). But it seems wrong to conclude this from merely being able to draft common principles. Whether jurisdictions resemble one another only becomes clear if all the relevant factors are taken into consideration. In doing so, it may be more important to find uniformity in the use of similar arguments than in common rules or case decisions: a common *text* will necessarily be interpreted in different ways in different countries.

An example of how identical arguments are weighed in different ways concerns the question of whether a non-performing contracting party has the right to a second chance, that is, to cure its performance. This is the case in German law: where there is late or deficient performance, the creditor is, in principle, only allowed to terminate the contract (§ 323 BGB) or claim damages in lieu of performance (§ 281 BGB) if he gave the debtor a period of notice to repair his previous non-performance. This means that the debtor has a *Recht zur zweiten Andienung*: he did something wrong (delivered too late or performed defectively), but still has a second chance to repair his wrongdoing. With the revision of the German law of obligations in 2002, the German legislator thus explicitly strengthened the rights of the seller against the buyer, who already receives ample protection by way of European directives.

Dutch law does not recognize this right to a second chance to perform. Where there is non-performance, it is enough to show the default of the debtor. This means, for example, that if a time was set for performance, and this time has passed, the creditor can immediately claim damages. The only thing the creditor needs to do is to send an *omzettingsverklaring* (art. 6:87 BW): the written announcement that he now claims damages in lieu of performance. In the case of termination, a written statement that the contract is terminated suffices (art. 6:267 BW). This does of course not mean that it is impossible in Dutch law to set extra time for performance: the creditor has the option to do so, but the debtor has no *right* to it. In this respect, Dutch law is like the PECL, which holds in art. 8:106 that the creditor *may* fix an additional period for performance. This is a case of *Selbstbindung* by the creditor: the creditor binds himself and can therefore not claim performance or termination during the set period.

All in all, it can be concluded that German law goes further in protecting the debtor against the enforcement of remedies by the creditor than Dutch law. This leads me to the question, 'Which system can be considered the *better* one?' 'What are the policy reasons behind allowing the debtor a second chance to perform?' I think there are two. First, there is the binding force of contract: if a party is allowed a second chance to perform, the contract will remain binding for a longer period of time. This is in line with the idea that once a contract is made, it should be upheld as long as possible and there have to be very good reasons to terminate or to claim damages instead of the specified performance. The mere passing of a fatal date may not then be enough. Secondly – and related to the first argument – the possibility of a rather quick termination, or allowing a damages claim, may lead to all kinds of complications. The amount of damages has to be assessed and, if the contract was already partly executed, the performance needs to be redressed, which can be difficult. This means there is an important incentive for the parties to simply perform instead of entering into these difficult questions.

The next logical question is whether there are any arguments against a right to cure the malperformance. One is the moral argument that the debtor did something wrong when he failed to perform in a timely manner and that this in itself should allow the creditor to claim damages or (under certain circumstances) termination of the contract. The Dutch legislator considered the adoption of the second chance to perform, but rejected it for exactly this reason. He also stated that Dutch legal practice would favour the possibility of the creditor immediately suing the debtor. However, it can be doubted whether this is really true. According to the case law of the Dutch Supreme Court (*e.g. Hoge Raad* 4 February 2000, NJ 2000, 258 (*Kinheim/Penders*)), the right of the debtor 'to try again' is seen as important. Also, the European directive 1999/44 on the sale of consumer goods gives the seller the right to repair or replace them. This seems to be evidence of a tendency to allow a contracting party to correct his or her mistakes. Another reason why the Dutch legislator refused to allow the debtor a second chance to perform was that the alternative was 'simpler'. However, this is difficult to see: a system in which the creditor first needs to set extra time for performance before he can claim damages or termination is not necessarily more complicated. See Smits (2008b).

Weighing identical arguments thus leads to different outcomes. However, the temptation must be resisted to distil an abstract principle from this, which can only lead to what Clifford Geertz once called a 'skeletonization of fact': a dilemma is then reduced to an abstraction for the sake of finding consensus. This is – in the vivid language of Lawrence Friedman (Legrand 1997, 59) – as if one 'took fields of living law, scalded off their flesh, drained off their blood, and reduced them to bones'.

43. When Should There Be Uniformity of Law?

The mere fact that the application of rules or principles will lead to different outcomes in different jurisdictions should indeed be a reason to speak about uniformity. Rather, the use of similar arguments is the criterion to judge legal uniformity.

The question of when exactly legal uniformity comes into existence can be answered in different ways. Thus, one can find uniformity in rules and in how these are applied by the courts. This means that, in order to be able to speak of uniformity, the law must consist of similar rules being applied in a uniform way throughout the European Union. However, this is a problematic criterion because such convergence does not even exist at the national level: different judges within one country can decide a similar case in different ways. And yet, this type of convergence is often meant when legal unification is being discussed in the European context. The provisions of the PECL and DCFR are written to help in achieving this type of convergence by way of rules. A lower level of unification is aimed at if commonalities are sought in principles or fundamental rights. A third possible criterion is whether the applied rules or achieved outcomes are *functionally* similar. Uniform law then exists if an identical goal (for example protection of the consumer or prevention of unfair competition) is achieved.

I believe that there ought to be another criterion in this discussion, which is whether different jurisdictions use similar arguments. In this respect, it is not relevant whether these arguments are given different weights (see also *supra*, no. 42). For example, it does not matter if German law regards a given prescription period as absolute while Dutch law does not if there is evidence of exceptional circumstances. It also does not matter that views of the legality of 'dwarf tossing' differ amongst jurisdictions (see *supra*, respectively, no. 33 and no. 36) so long as, in giving a judgment, all relevant arguments were weighed.

This view fits in well with the experience of the only real common law system that exists at present: that of England and its former colonies. Within common law countries, there is already a strong sense that the type of reasoning defended above is conducive to legal development. In particular, courts within the British Commonwealth tend to be inspired by arguments used by their foreign colleagues (see Smits 2006), even though this does not imply that the common law is identical everywhere. In the New-Zealand case of *Invercargill City Council* v. *Hamlin* ([1996] 2 WLR 367), the Privy Council noted that the common law can differ, dependent on 'general patterns of socio-economic behaviour'. Lord Lloyd of Berwick claimed that 'the ability of the common law to adapt itself to the differing circumstances of the countries in which it has taken root, is not a weakness, but one of its great strengths'. This led the court to conclude that the concept of *negligence* received a different meaning in the law of New Zealand than in English law.

This emphasis on arguments is also the core of the common European legal tradition of the *ius commune* as it existed before the national codifications of the nineteenth century. This *ius commune* never sought uniformity of rules, but was characterized by a method focused on finding the best outcome, using a not so clearly defined pool of rules, principles and arguments. Based on these predispositions, Roman law was used as a source, not because there was any compelling duty to do so, but because the solutions offered were seen as having informative value in arriving at the right decision. This is also why, if contemporary sources could contribute better to the goal of reaching the best outcome, they were given precedence over the received Roman law. This made the method pre-eminently an international one: there is no reason whatsoever to assume that arguments brought forward elsewhere would be of less importance than those accepted in one's own country.

It was rare in the *ius commune* tradition for there to be a strict duty to apply a certain rule to a case: how could it be otherwise when the available materials were partly contradictory? In other words, people drew inspiration from the rules that were seen to be best for dealing with the case before the court. Roman law offered an extensive inventory of solutions to legal problems but the insights of contemporary authors were also used if this was found to be useful. The way in which Derek van der Merwe (1996, 356) defines the jurist in a mixed jurisdiction was also true for the *ius commune*. He states that as an 'instinctive eclectic: [the jurist] will seek authority in the grand manner, the process of distilling legal wisdom largely uninhibited by rigid doctrinal boundaries. Such a state of mind is conducive to an unfussy flexibility in the application of the law.' See, with many details, Smits (2002a, 158 ff.). Having said this, we can only concur with Zimmermann (1997, 293): 'The essential prerequisite for a truly European private law would appear to be the emergence of an "organically progressive" legal science, which would have to transcend the national boundaries and to revitalize a common tradition.' The way to do this is to search for arguments used in the European jurisdictions.

44. Emphasis on Deciding Cases; Practical Wisdom

It was emphasized in the section above that, in law, principles and arguments will always conflict and that the academic method should therefore consist of the identification and rethinking of the relevant arguments. This makes it important to ask how, *in practice,* choices should be made so that one argument prevails over the other. This is also important for legal science: although it is not the primary task of legal academics to decide actual cases, one can expect that they will demonstrate how to do this in the specific normative setting of a jurisdiction.

The point of departure is what was earlier mentioned (for example, in no. 33) about the situation sense of the law: what ought to be in the actual case, can never be captured by rules or principles. The true decision will lie in balancing conflicting arguments: everyone accepts general principles such as equality, freedom of contract and protection of property, but what these principles really mean and how they conflict with each other only becomes clear when they are applied to a real case. This insight should lead to a re-evaluation of the law as *practical wisdom*. This view of the law, which disappeared over the horizon in the last few centuries due to the influence of the methodology of social and natural science, best fits the core activity of the jurist.

Practical wisdom (*phronesis* in Aristotle's *Nicomachean Ethics*) is the intellectual virtue of establishing what to do and which goals to achieve. In the work of Aristotle, it is distinct from *sophia*, which is concerned with universal truths (theoretical wisdom). Practical wisdom emphasizes that every case is unique and that it takes an experienced person to deal with it. Whilst *sophia* is only reflective, practical wisdom gives pride of place to the actual making of a choice and to the arguments which are decisive in doing this. Wisdom can be found in the many cases that have been decided in the past but not so much in abstract rules and principles.

Inspiration for a characterization of legal activity as practical wisdom can be found in the work of Stephen Toulmin, Alasdair MacIntyre and Martha Nussbaum. They all show how, before the rise of rational positivism, methods existed to balance values against each other in actual cases and how these methods made way for a more reductionist model of judgment-making in the seventeenth century under the influence of the rational positivist paradigm of knowledge. Toulmin (1990, 30) captures the prevailing academic method of the last 300 years well: 'Formal logic was in, rhetoric was out, general principles were in, particular cases were out, abstract axioms were in, concrete diversity was out, the permanent was in, the transitory was out.' This led to 'moral algebra', the almost mathematical balancing of values.

This narrative is consistent with how Schröder (2001, 23) describes legal science: until the Enlightenment, the emphasis was on *finding* the right solution (*inventio*) and making use of catalogues of important viewpoints (*topoi*). The successful book, *Topica Iuris, Sive Loci Argumentorum Legales* of 1516 is well known. In it Nicolas Everaerts discusses more than 100 such arguments. Around 1700, the use of *topoi*, as a way of determining the right outcome, was largely discarded to make way for systematization. Systematization, however, had its own limitations because the legal system can never, in and of itself, offer results.

Now is the fitting time for accepting (again) that choices among conflicting arguments can only be made in a practical way. Nussbaum (1986) and MacIntyre (1981) rightly emphasize that the weighing of interests is only possible in a real case and that any more abstract rules necessarily have a 'rule-of-thumb' character. People do not make practical choices on the basis of abstract truths or, as Holmes (1870, 1) stated: 'it is the merit of the common law that it decides the case first and determines the principle afterwards'. This fits in with the plea that social sciences should no longer be led by scientific methods, but should be practised primarily as *phronetic social science*. This view was expressed by Bent Flyvbjerg (2001) who shows that, although social scientists have long applied the idealisms of the natural sciences in their studies, this has not led to the ability to explain or predict social reality. Social scientists should therefore do what they are good at, instead, which is to engage in the normative discussion about which values our society should strive for and how to accomplish these goals. In other words, in order to become relevant again, social sciences should inform us about practical reason.

If legal practice is seen as a special form of applying practical wisdom, this may mean that the decision-making process itself is not transparent. The mere reference to the experience ('wisdom') of the legal decision-maker does not reveal how this decision is made and that may invoke the criticism that the decision is, in the end, nothing but a 'mystery'. It will become clear in no. 45 *infra* that this reproach is not justified.

It may be surprising that Richard Posner (2003, 64) also recognizes that in a pragmatist view of law, the ultimate criterion for the court is reasonableness: 'There is no algorithm for striking the right balance between rule-of-law and case-specific consequences (. . .). In fact, there isn't too much more to say to the would-be pragmatic judge than make the most reasonable decision you can, all things considered'. Cf. Menand (1997).

45. The Importance of Legal Doctrine

Practical wisdom depends to a large extent on the mature, yet subjective, view of the person making the decision. It is usually assumed that practical wisdom should also rest on a source of knowledge that is external to the decision-maker. As previously indicated (no. 39), doctrine (including previously decided cases) can fulfil this role in the empirical-normative approach, provided that it is regarded as providing empirical materials on how to deal with conflicting arguments.

It would be going too far to consider at this point the extensive (philosophical) discussion about how to underpin practical wisdom. However, one important school claims that it is vital for practical wisdom to make use of external sources in establishing what it entails. Thus, John Finnis (1997, 221) refers to morality and Millgram (1997, 161) to experience. Hsieh provides an overview of the discussion (2011).

Doctrine ('dogmatics') can be seen as representing the normative complexity of the law: the thousands of rules and decided cases, each with their own nuances, show the many ways in which the law can deal with conflicting values. Doctrine thus reflects how subtle the law can often be and why a small change in the facts can lead to a wholly different outcome. The elaboration of the doctrinal system is therefore not an etheric activity unconnected to reality, but an essential part of a legal activity aiming to capture the subtleness of the law in words.

It must be repeated that the question of whether an argument can be accepted within a particular jurisdiction can only be answered in that jurisdiction's normative context (see *supra*, no. 40). Doctrine thus enlightens us about the prevailing normative approaches. It is therefore no coincidence that, despite fierce attacks from several corners of academia, doctrine did survive. S.D. Smith (1992, 629) states: 'Indeed, to suggest that legal scholarship should be less obsessed with doctrine would be like suggesting that historians should not spend so much effort studying things that happened in the distant past, or that astronomers ought to worry more about earthly concerns instead of concentrating so exclusively on remote heavenly bodies.' Each argument must be passed through the filter of the legal system before it can be accepted: the legal activity consists in great measure in *feeling out* the system, turning each rule into a rule of thumb, and each previous decision into a possible example of how to decide the case in question. This is no easy task, and even if it may seem easy initially, a competent lawyer will *make* it difficult, not to keep himself busy but because he knows that subtle nuances are relevant. Singer (2009, 938) puts it like this: 'law is complicated because qualitative distinctions matter, and they matter at this level of detail'.

Legal doctrine not only fulfils a role as a source of practical wisdom, but it has two other functions as well. First, it creates

> a shared framework of texts, concepts and categories, without which a debate is not even possible. This is not only recognized in Europe (see, for example, Jansen 2005, 755), but also elsewhere. Tiller & Cross (2006, 1) rightly claim that 'legal doctrine is the currency of the law'. Many legal questions cannot even exist without a doctrinal system. Thus, the question of whether a security right in a moveable asset ('pledge') must be registered or whether constitutional review is available cannot be answered without a legal framework. In this respect, doctrine *creates* the legal reality (cf. *supra*, no. 9).
>
> Secondly, a doctrinal system can add to the coherence and lucidity of the law. The well-known criticism of the Critical Legal Studies movement (Unger 1986 and Kennedy 1976, 1685) that a doctrinal system has no other value than to disguise underlying contradictions is therefore far-fetched.

As a result, the normative activity of the legal scholar will consist of two steps. First, the relevant arguments for and against a certain solution need to be identified and reconsidered by making use of the empirical-normative method. Secondly, one can consider how these arguments fit into an existing normative setting (for example, a national jurisdiction). It is difficult to judge this in the abstract: the most convincing argument in the United States is not necessarily the same one as in Germany.

46. Which Argument Prevails? Comparison Without a *Tertium*

There is still another aspect of practical wisdom that needs attention. Comparison plays a fundamental role in the view of doctrine as empirical material in dealing with conflicting arguments. Such comparisons can take place at different levels. Thus, the decision for one argument to prevail over another in a particular case can be based on a comparison of similar cases. At a more abstract level, the acceptance of rules (or even of a whole normative system) can be made dependent on how to value this system in comparison with others.

Jonsen & Toulmin (1988, 34) characterize very well the importance of comparison in the approach developed above (that it does not search for the truth in a coherent and axiomatic system, but in the experience laid down in actual decisions about unique situations): 'Practical arguments depend for their power on how closely the present circumstances resemble those of the earlier precedent cases for which this particular type of argument was originally devised. So, in practical arguments, the truths and certitudes established in the precedent cases pass sideways, so as to provide "resolutions" of later problems (. . .).'

Scholars of comparative law tend to stipulate that any meaningful comparison must be based on some objective criterion (the so-called *tertium comparationis*). The (still prevailing) functional comparative method is based on this idea. However, if the functional measure of the comparison is sought in a criterion that is external to the law (such as utility or welfare), it is still a non-normative factor that is used to determine the 'better' jurisdiction. This is at odds with the idea that practical wisdom makes use of existing experience in judging an argument in a *legal* way. It is equally problematic that the functional approach brings diverse views of what people ought to do as a matter of law back to one common denominator. We saw earlier (for example, in no. 34) that this is impossible. The literature on pluralism of values shows that alternatives can be compared without having to fall back on some neutral measure.

In no. 15 *supra*, I have already argued that comparison without a *tertium comparationis* is entirely possible, for example, by way of a 'comparative second-order language'. This would even be necessary if no universal and absolutely valid value existed to which all arguments can be reduced. As Schroeder (2002) writes: 'No single metric can capture the rich diversity of values'. See also Nussbaum (1995, 14). This value pluralism presupposes that many different values and goals are worth aiming for, but that this can also lead to many conflicts among them, as in Isaiah Berlin's (1969) classic example of rival positive and negative liberty. This can make it difficult to choose: 'There is an objective moral order, but our perception of it is such that we cannot bring rival moral truths into complete harmony with each other. To choose does not exempt me from the authority of the claim which I choose to go against' (MacIntyre, 1981, 143). This is expressed more vividly in Simon & Garfunkel's 'Mrs. Robinson' (1967): 'When you've got to choose, | Ev'ry way you look at it, you lose'.

Various authors have considered how, despite the existence of incommensurable values, one is able to reason in favour of one alternative or the other. Even if values cannot be measured on the basis of one common standard, alternative solutions can still be positively compared with each other. Hsieh (2011) gives an overview of proposed solutions on how to do this. For the legal discipline, Jonsen & Toulmin (1988, 330) show how the case at hand can be compared with previously decided paradigm cases. Ronald Dworkin's (1986) view of common law jurisprudence as a chain novel also implies that comparison is possible without making use of an explicit external measure by finding analogies in a more subtle way. Lawyers, consciously or not, practise these insights on a daily basis. See also Dannemann (2006, 396ff.), with reference to John Stuart Mill's 'method of agreement' and 'method of difference'.

3. CONCLUSIONS

47. Summary

This chapter started by asking how to determine what one is legally obliged to do if one cannot have recourse to the authority of legislatures and courts. It was argued in the sections above that there is no one answer to this question and that the core of the academic study of law (at least in the normative approach) consists of showing time and again that one can dispute in perpetuity about what ought to be. The realm of legal science consists then of identifying and re-thinking arguments, and of demonstrating how these arguments might fit the normative setting of a specific jurisdiction. The accompanying method is the empirical-normative one: existing jurisdictions can be seen as laboratories for how to manage conflicting normative positions. The eventual adoption of one argument as the stronger can only take place in the context of a particular jurisdiction. The way in which this decision is made is best described as an application of practical wisdom.

This plea will of course not be accepted if one believes that the law is a question of authority and is only binding because of the institutional place of the legislature and courts. See Collier (1991, 194). However, what Geoffrey Samuel (2008, 314) claims about comparative lawyers is, in my view, true for any jurist: they must work 'within a spirit of enquiry rather than authority'.

48. Normative Scholarship as an Academic Discipline

In no. 21 *supra,* three requirements were identified that any academic discipline should meet. Academic work does not only aim for the systematization of knowledge, but this knowledge must also have been obtained by a method that is recognized as valid by the academic community and must supersede that of a local authority. The question must now be answered to what extent normative legal scholarship meets these requirements.

No. 22 *supra* discussed how far the other (non-normative) types of legal science discussed in Chapter I can meet the requirements of an academic discipline. The mere fact that normative uncertainty is an important characteristic of the law does not mean that academic work in law cannot meet these requirements. Uncertainty does not rule out a rational approach or, as Singer (2009, 929) says: 'Perhaps reason can coexist with controversy.'

It is beyond doubt that normative legal science can meet the first requirement. The proposed approach gives pride of place to the extension of the existing arsenal of legal knowledge: instead of formulating and interpreting national rules, the emphasis is on the identification of arguments and on investigating how these are weighed in different jurisdictions. This empirical material is stored in tens of thousands of rules and judicial decisions. This does imply, however, that we must search for new structures to categorize these arguments: the present systematic divisions along the lines of national legal systems must be abandoned.

Normative legal science can also meet the second requirement: legal science forms not only an academic practice (see *supra*, no. 21), but it can also adopt a clear research method by way of the proposed empirical-normative method that was explained above (no. 39). This requires a shift in perspective: case law and legislation should not be considered as sources of what the positive law says, but as empirical material about the strengths and weaknesses of certain normative arguments.

Finally, the renewed attention to arguments means that legal science is no longer dependent on national law but has the potential to become a truly international discipline. It would be wrong to find the universal character of the legal discipline at the level of rules (as is the case in many projects in the field of European private law). This falsely suggests that these rules – with their pretence of being applicable – can be understood in the same way throughout Europe.

In some fields, such as those of European private law and European constitutional law, an extensive international debate already exists. It is clear that in the view defended in this book, academic debate preferably takes place in English: if one's aim is to identify and reflect upon arguments, one is not bound by national borders or by one's own language. See also *infra*, no. 62.

IV. Organization of the legal-academic discourse

1. INTRODUCTION

49. Debate about Organization

I commented in the Introduction that the present discussion of legal scholarship is not only about its aims and methods; it also deals with the way in which universities organize their research and teaching, assess their researchers, and classify their journals. In this debate, there is often a surprising lack of awareness about the place of legal scholarship in comparison to other disciplines. It is also not uncommon for views of how the legal discipline should evolve to be primarily determined by concerns about its quality and funding, rather than by substantive issues.

> In the Netherlands (cf. Stolker 2003 and 2005), the debate about the academic aspirations of legal science was boosted by a concern to defend legal research against other disciplines that do not take it seriously enough. However, the themes discussed in this chapter are not unique to legal research: many of the trends mentioned below can be found in other academic disciplines as well (such as the debate about methodology) or even in society as a whole (the turn towards 'market thinking').

This last chapter discusses several questions surrounding the organization of legal discourse. The views expressed follow partly from the view of legal scholarship that was defended in the previous sections, but it will also contain an independent analysis of the matter, equally taking into consideration types of legal research different from the normative variant (see *supra*, no. 5).

The consequences of my proposed view of legal scholarship for aspects other than the organization of research are omitted from this book – even though these consequences do exist. One important result of the law being about conflicting normative positions lies, for example, in the organization of the highest courts: it can be argued that a system of concurring and dissenting opinions would lead to better argumentation than a system in which the court speaks with only one voice. The argument that introducing dissenting opinions would not be conducive to collegiality, as the President of the Dutch Supreme Court Geert Corstens recently noted (Lindo 2009, 1078), seems an admission of weakness. Allowing the well-argued views of fellow judges to be heard could lead to a more open discussion among judges and in society, in particular, when there are controversial decisions. See Smith (2009) on the close link between allowing dissenting opinions and a jurisdiction's aversion to bureaucratic authority.

If legal scholarship is characterized as a permanent debate without any definitive answers about what people ought to do as a matter of law, the first question to be addressed is what this means for the legal discipline in terms of what it contributes to making progress, and how legal academics can carry out creative research. This question is discussed in Section 2, followed by a discussion of the question of the methodology of legal science and the extent to which the legal discipline has its own character in Section 3. This opens up the way for a discussion in Section 4 about the academic culture in law and how best to organize legal research and teaching.

2. INNOVATION IN LEGAL SCIENCE

50. The Importance of Creativity

The prestige of any academic discipline is to a large extent determined by innovators and by the degree to which their new ideas are appreciated by the community of scholars. Academic success is then measured by the passionate propagation of one's own ideas and by the extent to which others follow in the footsteps of the innovators. This is also the case in legal scholarship: in every episode of its history, we can point to individuals who challenged existing knowledge and were subsequently followed by others. Many of the present concepts, rules and methods used in the field of law today are the past works of creative jurists. This notion of law as a man-made product ought to be emphasized more in legal education.

I can only refer here to some striking examples in the limited field of private law (and without elaborate reference to sources). There has been an influx of generally adopted legal 'inventions' (see Hoeren 2001) and it is difficult to imagine the legal field without them. The concept of the 'legal act' (*Rechtsgeschäft*) is a clear example of a legal institution that was invented by Von Savigny in order to facilitate legal thinking (see also *supra*, no. 8). Notions such as offer, acceptance, and obligation also received their present, well-defined, meaning within a system of private law only as a result of the work of the Pandectists. Even the idea that it is useful to systematize the law at all was (under the influence of Humanism) 'invented' in the sixteenth and seventeenth century thanks to innovators such as Donellus, Leibniz, Pufendorf and Wolff. The work of Von Savigny (1814 [1831, 30]) is also important because he caused a shift in the paradigm: law does not follow from reason, but is developed first 'by custom and popular faith, next by jurisprudence'. He was equally influential in making explicit the methods of statutory interpretation (grammatical, logical, historical and systematic) that exist (cf. Stein 2000, 13). Another innovation, namely, that the application of law must primarily be tailored to the interests of the actual case, can be derived from Von Jhering. Present-day innovators no longer tend to come from Germany but from the United States: without the pioneering work of Ronald Coase, Guido Calabresi and Richard Posner, the insight that the law can also be viewed from the economic perspective would not have been accepted. Duncan Kennedy's critical approach towards the law is of equal importance. More recently, Steven Levitt gave a whole new impetus to the empirical approach to law (see *supra*, no. 16).

It is striking (if not disappointing for the state of the legal discipline) that revolutionary innovators often feel it better not to reveal their true names to the legal community. This was true for Von Jhering who, in 1861, published his accusations against the prevailing *Begriffsjurisprudenz* anonymously in the form of confidential letters. In 1906, soon after the introduction of the German Civil Code, Kantorowicz waged war against existing legist judicial practice in The Battle for Legal Science under the pseudonym Gnaeus Flavius. Around the turn of the twentieth century in South Africa, the battle over the thorny question of whether to adopt English law or Roman-Dutch law was also fought under fictitious names (see Smits 2002a, 165ff.).

It is difficult to overestimate the importance of innovative research. In particular, the academic work that takes place at universities ought to challenge existing knowledge and offer new perspectives. Any researcher worth his salt ought to be driven primarily by his intellectual curiosity, motivated by his desire to discover something new, and to be fearless in the face of challenging the establishment. Just like the first wave of abstract painters or atonal composers, gifted researchers must strive not simply to imitate their predecessors, but to attempt to create something new. To advocate otherwise would be the literary equivalent of wishing that such diverse authors as De Sade, Robbe-Grillet and Coetzee wrote about the same subjects in the same way. Unfortunately, it is not the standard view of the layman or first year student that legal science offers just as many possibilities for this as astrophysics or neuroscience does. On the contrary, the common opinion seems to be that getting to know the law and its system should go hand in hand with abandoning an inquisitive attitude. Studying law often means that one learns about the certainties of a legal system without asking how things could be done differently. This does not match the intellectual challenge that legal questions can offer.

Cf. Posner (1990, 431–432). Also, the Amsterdam professor Ad Lagendijk (1997) emphasizes that in physics 'doing things that are against current practice' will lead to winning Nobel Prizes. In my view, a good researcher is therefore contrarian and writes, as was once said about Richard Posner, 'not to defend, but to be accused'. In Posner's view, the doctrinal approach no longer meets the requirement of originality: to fit new legislation and judicial decisions into a doctrinal system comes, in his view, too close to legal practice and is now 'work for followers rather than leaders', if it is not 'old-fashioned, passé, tired'. In my view, the problem lies not so much in the doctrinal approach itself, which can also be creative, for example when it arranges the existing materials in a given field anew (see also the examples given in no. 8 *supra*). Rather, this type of research is derivative since it does not pose its own questions but rather prefers to comment on decisions taken by the authoritative institutions. Instead, the researcher should have his own agenda (cf. Rubin 1988, 1883 and Vranken 2006, 115ff.).

51. Innovative Research: Many Types

Although the great importance of creative research has now been established, the question of what exactly is creative must still be addressed. In my view, research into law can be creative in many different ways. It would be wrong to consider one type as being better than another. In an important article, Mathias Siems recently showed many of the different ways legal research can be considered to be original.

Siems (2008) provides an exuberant overview of what can be defined as original research in law by categorizing it into four different types. First, micro-legal questions analyse a specific legal problem that flows from, for example, a statute, a code or a court decision. They can aim for a new analysis of an existing problem or provide it with an original solution. The originality can thus lie in different things: in finding coherence within the national legal system from which the question arises (such as the 'discovery' of the reliance principle in German law by Canaris: see *supra*, no. 8 and Hoeren 2001, 377ff.); or of the principle of proportionality in European law (Van Gerven 1999), but also in showing how a national solution relates to a foreign solution (as in comparative law), or to a previously existing solution (as in legal history), or how it fits a certain philosophical or economic view of law.

Legal questions can also be original in addressing issues at the macro level (Siems 2008, 152): at this level, research is not about a specific problem related to a statute or case but is concerned with general concepts, problems and principles. Examples include, but are not limited to: developing new philosophical foundations of law (as in the work of John Rawls and Ronald Dworkin); determining what is the province and method of legal science; answering the question how European private law may best be designed, and whether open-ended or specific norms are better for legal development. Writing a new textbook on contract law or on the law of criminal procedure in which the law is described in a new and coherent way (or in which a lack of coherence is demonstrated) is equally original.

The two other types of original legal research distinguished by Siems (2008, 156ff.) are closer to other academic fields and are therefore more often practised by non-lawyers. Empirical Law and Economics (dealing with the effects of a legal rule on social welfare) is an example of this, as is the previously discussed work (no. 16) of Levitt & Donohue (2001) on the influence of the legalization of abortion on crime. On the other hand, it is possible to research a more general theme, law being only one of the factors taken into consideration. This is the case if one explains a societal phenomenon, such as the factors contributing to a high crime rate in a particular country, where the law is only one of the factors being considered alongside other factors including, but not limited to, the average level of education, income and composition of the population.

It must be emphasized here that one type of innovative research (such as analysis at the micro level) is not necessarily better than another (such as empirical work). Universities and funding organizations sometimes tend to refer to certain types of research as having more quality than others when pursuing their own managerial priorities but this is not entirely accurate or even fair: there is nothing against individual law faculties or funding agencies deliberately choosing to promote a certain type of research, but they should not use the argument that only a certain type is of sufficient quality. See also *infra*, no. 61.

52. Is there Progress in Legal Science?

The next important question is whether creativity in legal scholarship can also lead to progress. In the 'hard' disciplines, in which the significance of innovative research is invariably emphasized, the standard view of science is that the total amount of knowledge increases with new discoveries. However, the picture of accumulating knowledge – implying that the views of predecessors are rejected and replaced by new insights in a sometimes revolutionary way – only seems applicable to fields characterized by clear paradigms. Legal science – at least in its normative variant – does not have such a core of undisputed knowledge (and hence an idea of what counts as progress compared to this core). As Thomas Kuhn put it: contrary to a 'normal' scientist, a student of the humanities is confronted with a variety of problems and 'has constantly before him a number of competing and incommensurable solutions to tackle these problems, solutions that he must ultimately evaluate for himself'. This makes it difficult, if not impossible, to judge if there is any progress in the sense of the natural sciences.

See Kuhn (1970, 165). The idea of scientific progress (and, as a consequence not only development, but also an improvement of the law) is closely associated with the rational positivism of the seventeenth century (see *supra*, no. 44), where new and better knowledge can be obtained through empirical testing. However, if empirical testing is impossible (as in legal science), we can no longer speak of progress. Even if it is proclaimed, that particular notion of progress will surely be scrutinized, if not contested. This is also the conclusion Volney Gay (2009) reached when he surveyed the question of progress in the humanities. His conclusion is that science and the humanities are fundamentally different, claiming that cultural objects can only be studied within their context and that the only 'progress' that can be made consists of giving new meanings to existing information.

On the absence of paradigms in the social sciences and humanities (and about how progress in hard sciences has taken place by way of revolutionary paradigm shifts), see Kuhn (1970). Once a paradigm (as a universally recognized set of scientific achievements that provides model problems and solutions for a community of researchers) has come into existence, all the rest is a matter of solving puzzles. This explains why natural science puts so much emphasis on formulating substantive research questions that are subsequently 'solved' within the paradigmatic standard model of, for example, physics (since the seventeenth century that model has essentially been rational positivism). It follows that the most interesting questions deal with the (in the Kuhnian sense) anomalies that do not fit into the established paradigm. In such cases, application of existing methods does not lead to a solution (as substantiated by the present debate among physicists over string theory). This is an important insight because legal academics and representatives of other disciplines sometimes talk at cross-purposes when discussing the role of method: see *infra*, no. 54.

Better than the term 'progress' – implying that out-dated insights have definitely been left behind – the neutral term 'evolution' reflects how development in legal science takes place. Changes happen in a process of competition in which only the useful arguments (or concepts or rules) survive. However, it is essential to normative legal science that legal institutions never become fully extinct: an argument, concept or rule that was useful in the past can become important again in the future, much like the way figurative artists made a come back following the first tide of abstract painters.

The evolutionary approach was explained *supra*, no. 27. This also means that any falsification of legal rules is not possible: if law is characterized as the discipline of conflicting arguments (see Chapter III above), the validity of these arguments cannot be refuted by courts or legislatures. The only possible conclusion is that a certain argument fits a given normative setting (such as a national jurisdiction) better, where better means that it is more strongly conducive to satisfying a goal that is external to the law (such as efficiency) or that it has more explanatory power (as the term 'legal act' may be useful in denoting a number of common effects of the different legal phenomena of a contract, a testament and the giving of notice). It is important to realize in this regard that Popper never applied the idea of falsification to the law or morals (Wendt 2008, 64); see also Ulen (2002, 9) and Jansen (2005, 772). What is more: falsification is not only impossible in law, it is also unnecessary. Whilst, in the empirical disciplines, only non-falsified hypotheses produce real knowledge, the jurist knows that the legal materials are never silent: one can always find arguments for and against a certain solution.

The non-cumulative character of legal science has yet another consequence. In disciplines that build upon existing knowledge, it is usually not very difficult to identify the questions that are still open. A first year student of mathematics or astronomy, for example, can immediately list several problems that his discipline is wrestling with that, at some point in time, could be 'solved'. Normative legal scholarship is fundamentally different. First, the law does not have any unsolvable questions because the existing materials always allow at least some solution. But more importantly, the accuracy of this solution can be continuously subjected to debate and scrutiny. Innovations in legal science, therefore, are produced through the weighing of different arguments from varying perspectives.

Mathematics offers an example of an (at least until recently) unsolved problem: the proof of the so-called Poincaré conjecture (formulated in 1904): 'Anything that looks spherical, is spherical', or 'every simply connected, closed 3-manifold is homeomorphic to the 3-sphere'. In 2002, the eccentric Russian mathematician Grisja Perelman proved the conjecture and promptly received the Fields Medal (see *infra*, no. 60), which he just as promptly declined to accept. Such a discovery is inconceivable in law: at best, an argument that was used in the past prevails under new circumstances or in a changed society. Although these arguments can also come from other disciplines outside the legal field, as was previously noted (see *supra*, no. 37), how exactly particular non-legal knowledge is important in answering the normative question should always be detailed fully.

This does not of course suggest that legal researchers should not explicitly specify how new research relates to what was done in the past. Legal academics at universities too often reproduce only what others did before them. It is important for them to make explicit what new insights follow from their research.

3. LEGAL SCIENCE AND METHODOLOGY

53. Introduction

Much attention has been paid recently to the research methods used by legal academics. This interest is partly caused by intellectual curiosity ('What do we do as legal scholars and, in particular, how do we do it?'), but it is partly prompted by practical purposes as well. The logic behind the practical reasons is as follows: practitioners of other disciplines can, more often than not, indicate precisely which method(s) they use in doing research, unlike legal academics, who too often continue to refrain from doing so at the risk of losing money and prestige in the battle among disciplines.

Increased attention to the methodology of legal science can be seen in various countries. See, for Germany, Engel & Schön (2007) and Bernhart (2008), for the UK, McCrudden (2006), and for the Netherlands, Van Gestel & Vranken (2011, 925ff.) and Vranken (2006, 94): 'What is the subject of the research, and why? How does it relate to existing research? (. . .) What are the best methods to conduct the research?' See also Van Hoecke (2011). In the United States, Epstein & King (2002, 11) advanced a similar plea, though the scope of their conclusion was limited to the situation in which jurists do empirical research: 'The law is important enough to have a subfield devoted to methodological concerns, as does almost every other discipline that conducts empirical research.' Cf. Rhode (2002).

Particularly in the eyes of other disciplines' representatives, legal academics often make use of an unclear methodology. This becomes apparent in assessing research proposals by funding organizations such as the Deutsche Forschungsgemeinschaft (DFG), the UK's Economic and Social Research Council (ESRC) and Arts and Humanities Research Council (AHRC),

> and the Dutch Nederlandse Organisatie voor Wetenschappelijk Onderzoek (NWO). All these funding organizations (like also the Directorate for Social, Behavioural & Economic Sciences (SBE) of the US National Science Foundation) increasingly assess proposals for research grants in interdisciplinary panels that consist not only of jurists, but also of economists, psychologists and other academics. In the Dutch situation, the assessment is indeed taking place at an increasingly high level. Before 1995, law had its own panel within the division of the social sciences but, since then, the barriers that separated the academic fields into various divisions have been levelled. The aim was explicitly to unify the assessment procedure, to refrain from adhering to mechanisms that protected certain fields, and to stimulate interdisciplinary work. The result is that jurists now have to compete with not only economists and psychologists, but also with sociologists, anthropologists and colleagues working in political science and management studies. Although there are clear advantages to breaking down these disciplinary walls, the problem persists that lawyers have a hard time convincing colleagues in other fields of the soundness of their methodology.

The first question addressed in this section is whether the use of clear research methods can have the same effect in law that it has in the empirical disciplines and, if not, what alternatives exist (no. 54). Subsequently, a plea is made for a better justification of choices made in legal research (no. 55), but also for putting into perspective the importance of an explicit research question (no. 56), as well as for a methodological pluralism, which states that one method is not, in and of itself, better than another (no. 57). The development that disciplines such as economics and psychology have endured will illustrate why any other view regarding this matter is a mere delusion.

54. Research Methods and Law

If a method is a way to achieve a predetermined goal, then a research method is a way to provide rules on how to conduct research: it indicates how knowledge is to be acquired in order to answer a question. This implies that a research method presupposes two things: there must be a question that deserves to be answered; and the answer to this question will only be viewed as reliable if a particular method has been followed. To 'coincidentally' find the right answer does not suffice: the steps taken to reach the result must be verifiable to others. If this requirement of a verifiable method is taken seriously in legal scholarship, it means that only knowledge obtained through this method can be recognized as viable.

A method in the sense of generally accepted rules to achieve academic knowledge about the law must be distinguished from several other legal 'methods'. Thus, a method of 'legal thinking' is often mentioned (see Mastronardi 2001, Schauer 2009 and *supra*, no. 28), or similarly methods of finding the law (*Rechtsfindung*: the heuristics of legal reasoning) or of legitimating a decision. If (as is claimed in a still influential view) the activities of the legal scholar do not fundamentally differ from those of the judge, these methods of finding and legitimating the law are also to be seen as scholarly methods (thus e.g. Larenz 1991, 6ff.). Finally, there are the more practical methods ('skills'), such as how to find legislation, case law and literature and how to argue, cite sources and interpret legislative texts (on which, for example, in Germany Tettinger & Mann 2009, in France Bonnet 2006 and in the Netherlands IJzermans & Van Schaaijk 2007).

How far is legal scholarship also subject to this methodological requirement? This question can be justified because the idea that knowledge acquired by using a scientific method is more reliable than knowledge that is not, stems from the empirical disciplines. In the empirical disciplines, it is usually assumed that the results of a research must be verifiable and even replicable in order to disprove any notion that observation of the facts could lead to falsification or data tampering. There is even more reason to ask whether the legal discipline ought to be subject to a strict methodology in view of the fact that strict methodological requirements do not usually have to be met in the humanities and are, at least, disputed in the social sciences.

For Popper (2002) the qualification of an academic field as science is dependent on whether the method of falsification can lead to collecting knowledge. The use of this particular method is thus a criterion of demarcation: it allows us to distinguish between scientific (usually empirical) and other knowledge. This does not mean that in Popper's view, knowledge cannot be obtained in any other way, only that it is then not found by way of falsification. In several continental European countries, including the Netherlands, this view became influential outside the natural sciences through the work of Adriaan de Groot, whose book on the methodology of behavioural sciences in 1969 influenced generations of psychologists, sociologists, and others. De Groot emphasizes the importance of a rational scientific model in which the researcher must always formulate his views by way of testable hypotheses. He must subsequently test these in what he calls the 'empirical cycle': a research starts with the observation of empirical facts and a formulation of hypotheses, followed by empirical testing and evaluation of their theoretical validity. See on the methodology of the non-empirical disciplines also John & McIver Lopes (2004) and Leezenberg & De Vries (2001, 83).

In my view, the function of a method in normative legal scholarship cannot be the same as in the empirical disciplines. The latter use a method to ban all uncertainty: precisely because a certain method was followed, there can no longer be any doubt about the accuracy of the outcome. Anyone else following the same method will have to reach the same result. This is fundamentally different in normative legal scholarship: the use of any method will not banish doubt, instead – as was elaborately argued in Chapter III – it will lead to a new discussion. Put differently, the use of a particular method will not make the answer to normative questions more 'academic' and knowledge that is acquired by way of a certain method is not for this reason less disputed.

This does not mean that it is impossible to acquire objective or reliable knowledge in the legal discipline. It means, however, that knowledge is acquired in another way that is not strictly prescribed by research methods: the legal discipline is primarily a practice, in which the community of academic colleagues (the forum) decides on what is to be seen as reliable knowledge.

Knowledge can come about either because it was reached through some defined method, or because it is recognized in academic practice (cf. *infra*, no. 21). Together with many of the humanities and social sciences, normative legal scholarship can be seen as such a practice. Knowledge that is obtained within these fields is not inferior to empirical knowledge – it is only a different type of knowledge. This point is also made by Joseph William Singer (2009) when he tells us that normative argument need not be airtight to make it valuable. The prominent German author Karl Larenz (1991, 6–7) similarly shows that the objectivity of legal scholarship lies in its ability 'to further develop the existing value judgments, to make these explicit, and to relate any new value judgments that have to be made within certain limits to the existing ones'. The constraint here is that one cannot achieve the 'degree of certainty and preciseness as in mathematics or as in performing a physical experiment'.

The community of scholars deciding what is to be seen as objective knowledge (so-called 'disciplinary objectivity') is one of the 'cultures of objectivity' distinguished by Porter (1995, 3 ff.). This idea of a forum means that any insights must be part of a continuous discussion: even though the 'truth' of an insight cannot be established and there is, at best, consensus among academics that it is the right one – in much the same way as with the paradigms of Thomas Kuhn. The consensus must of course exist as to a certain view being defensible, but not that it is the only possible view. For example, Backhouse (1997, 41) considers an idea to be decisive if it was first proposed in an article, was subsequently discussed by others and is eventually mentioned in a textbook. This makes any academic discipline a 'self-correcting' process (Leezenberg & De Vries 2001, 17). See also Patterson (2001), emphasizing that what is considered objective and marked as reliable is completely dependent on the field in question.

55. Making Choices Explicit

In the previous section, reservations were expressed about the importance of clearly defined methods in doing normative legal research. This is not to suggest that it is useless for legal researchers to state the exact topic of their research explicitly (the 'research question'), why it takes place (the 'aim') and how the researcher approaches the theme (the 'method'). This follows from the need in any academic field to present research in a transparent and fair way, thus adding to the reliability and quality of the research results: in any writing about the law, choices are made and in so far as these are not self-evident to the academic community, making these choices explicit will help the researcher and its audience in making clear what the research is about.

Discussion about the methodology of legal research is often framed as a matter of quality: more attention to formulating a precise research question and an accompanying method to answer it, would lead to better research. However, as evidenced *infra*, no. 54, methodology is here characterized unjustifiably as having the same role that it has in the empirical sciences where methodology has the potential to distinguish between reliable and unreliable knowledge. Apart from that, this view suffers from the same problem of which methodologists have often accused legal scholars: a lack of empirical basis. It is difficult to establish empirically that research not based on a clear methodological foundation is of less quality than research based on a sound methodology. It seems, in any event, that today's legal academic community does not judge the quality of academic work in terms of the use of a clear research method, but places much more emphasis on peer review, favourable book reviews or the reputation of the author. See, for a similar view, the reactions to Epstein & King (2002) in the special issue of the *University of Chicago Law Review* 2002, no. 1.

Legal research is insufficiently explicit particularly when it comes to the discussion of how to evaluate a judicial decision or a piece of legislation. This assessment is often not based on the legal system itself (where the most important criterion is the way in which one element connects to the other elements of the system), but on some legal criterion that is difficult to measure ('the legal certainty', 'social justice', and so on) or even on a criterion that is based outside the law ('the interests of business parties', 'what works?'). It is then necessary to make explicit what this criterion precisely requires.

Similar views are expressed by Posner (2000, 69), Vranken (2006, 94 ff.) and Tijssen (2009, 75). The latter mentions, in this context, the importance of a framework of assessment. One could also wish that legal scholars were more careful when making statements about the effects of changes in the law, such as: the alleged drop in crime as a result of abortion legalization (see *infra*, no. 16); the increase in false confessions through the use of certain interrogation techniques; or about delays in civil procedure caused by changes in procedural law.

Epstein & King (2002, 38) are particularly critical of this type of 'empirical' research by academic lawyers. Their most important criticism is that the requirement of replicability is almost never met: 'Another researcher should be able to understand, evaluate, build on, and reproduce the research without any additional information from the author (. . .). Unfortunately, the present state of legal scholarship nearly always fails this most basic of tests.' To Epstein and King (who are both political scientists) the individuality of the researcher is completely irrelevant: 'sentences that begin "I think" or "I believe" are beside the point' (p. 45). However, in the empirical-normative approach advocated above (no. 39), the confrontation with empirical data can take place in a much more liberal way. These data are not used to discover the truth but are arguments that have already been tested in the practice of an existing jurisdiction. See also Shapin (2008, 6) on the idea of the 'invisible scientist' as argued by Epstein & King.

Traditional doctrinal research can also benefit from a better clarification of the questions it seeks to answer. The goal of this type of research is usually to mould new legislation and judicial decisions in the legal system, or to create a whole new system by categorizing the existing materials in a different way. However, these seemingly routine activities also require many choices to be made, such as over which materials are to be used (only those produced by the national authorities, or also European and foreign legislation and case law, or even private regulation), and how these are to be systematized.

This is because systematization is possible in different ways, as exemplified by the various approaches of Von Savigny (1840–1848 [1979]), Larenz (1991, 474ff.), Canaris (1983) and MacCormick (1978). In addition, the question of how to determine internal consistency within the legal system deserves some explication in this type of work.

It is important to emphasize that the goal of the research need not lie in solving a societal problem or in better understanding society. The consequence of this would be that law could only be studied as an instrument and not as an autonomous system (as is indeed suggested by Epstein & King 2002, 60). Tijssen (2009, 74ff.) rightly states that the framework of assessment can also consist of the legal system itself, such as when new materials are fitted into this system.

56. A Need for an Explicit Research Question?

Of course, the aforementioned conclusion does not suggest that a 'research problem' always needs to be rigidly designated, nor does it mean that it must follow an equally rigid description of its methods. As is also the case with good research in the humanities and social sciences, legal research often has rhetorical power: if the 'creative jurist' believes that his research cannot be presented after the model of the empirical disciplines, this is completely legitimate.

The most important reason why an explicit formulation of a problem should not be overvalued lies in the fact that the non-empirical disciplines do not test hypotheses. The humanities and the law are more often concerned with – in the wording of Ferdinand Feldbrugge – 'the investigation of a broader field, where, at least initially, no specific questions are asked, but a wider range of phenomena is observed and described. This procedure may then yield various alternative avenues for further research (. . .). The researcher is like a nineteenth century explorer who enters an area which is still blank on the available maps. He does not really know what he is looking for.'

> See Feldbrugge (2003, vii). He explains how, when he started working on his book, *The Law's Beginnings*, a clear-cut theme was missing. Initially, his interest was in doing 'something' with 'early law', dealing with issues such as: 'What happens during the phase of legal development in which law divests itself of its close relationship with other aspects of social life?' 'What are the conditions under which the law 'begins' to exist?' 'Are there parallels between archaic jurisdictions in India, Greece, Italy, Ireland, Friesland, Russia and Mesopotamia?' In other words, the exact question of the research only became clear after the research was done.
>
> The research that is seen as important by the academic community often follows the road laid out by Feldbrugge. Thus, such diverse works as John Rawls' *A Theory of Justice* (1999), Johannes Köndgen's *Selbstbindung ohne Vertrag* (1981) and Reinhard Zimmermann's *The Law of Obligations* (1990) do not have a clear research question. Ronald Coase's *The Problem of Social Cost* (1960), one of the most influential works in the field of Law and Economics, also does not pose a clear question: it merely describes at the outset what the article is about in the way promoted by Feldbrugge.

This does not mean that once the research is finalized, a research question can no longer be formulated. It does mean, however, that this can only be a justification afterwards of what the creative researcher – by reading, writing, reflecting and discussing – did, in fact. The research question, the sources to be used and the research theme form a trinity and, together, they are in constant development during the research. Of course, formulating a research question can be a useful tool, forcing the researcher to a first demarcation of the research theme. In many cases, putting the argument in the form of a question that is then subsequently answered can also have rhetorical power. But this is not the recipe for creative or high-quality research.

Leezenberg & De Vries (2001, 66) point out that the scheme of research question and method is only a 'reconstruction' of the research process by rational positivists and is unjustifiably seen as a recipe for the design of good research. This overlooks the fact that such schemes only deal with the justification of knowledge and not with its acquisition: requirements in the context of justification are not to be confused with requirements in the context of discovery. Put differently, if one is able to formulate a research question in the way prescribed by methodologists, it is likely that one already knows the answer. Carrying out research in this way may not give much pleasure; see for other objections also Backhouse (1997, 8ff.). The experience of any good researcher is that creative research (on the importance of which *supra*, no. 50) is often dictated by coincidental 'discoveries', done in libraries (and often not by looking into the books and journals that are directly related to the theme), on the internet, or flowing from discussions with colleagues (also from other disciplines) or students. The importance of browsing also condemns the complete replacement of 'paper' law journals to its electronic counterpart (cf. *infra*, no. 59).

Important discoveries in natural science often do not rise out of previously formulated hypotheses. This is certainly true for paradigm shifts (Kuhn 1970; Newton did not build upon Aristotle's *Physics*), but also for less revolutionary finds. Much more often, something is 'observed' by a trained academic who does not know precisely what he is looking for, but who – thanks to his 'practical wisdom' – sees how progress can be made. Leeuwenhoek did not discover the microscope because he was looking for it, and Gregory House MD does not make the right diagnosis because he follows some medical protocol. The good researcher must have space for what is sometimes called 'informed messing around' or 'unguided play': he must be allowed the freedom to fiddle around and see in the same materials what somebody else did not see.

57. Methodological Pluralism

Having read the considerations above, it will not come as a surprise that legal science can make use of many different methods and that one method is not necessarily better than the other. Which method must be used is completely dependent on the aim of the research. If one aims to fit existing materials into the legal system, one would have to make use of another method than if one intended to build up a new system. And someone interested in interpreting a judicial decision will go about answering this question in a different way from someone who wants to investigate the effects of the decision on the behaviour of individuals.

As indicated above (no. 55), it is fair for a critic or a reader of academic work to expect a full disclosure of the method used. This is a matter of transparency and, for similar reasons, a legal academic should not only state the arguments in favour of his position but also the arguments against it. In addition to this, the legal academic should be independent (that is, he does not have a professional, financial or private interest in arguing in a certain way) and be accurate in referring to his sources.

How important it is to preserve this pluralism of methods – hence not to completely trade in the legal methods for those of other disciplines – is proven by the development that economics and psychology have gone through in the last half-century. Both fields (or at least those parts that are seen as the most prestigious) now rely heavily on empirical and mathematical methods.

In the last fifty years, there has been a keen methodological battle in both disciplines. This led to a much debated victory of the mathematical method in economics (cf. Debreu 1991) and to an emphasis on cognitive models in psychology. What Nobel Prize winner, George Stigler, noted back in 1963 (1ff.) with regard to the dominance of the mathematical method in economics is representative of how many economists see this development: 'The age of quantification is now full upon us. We are now armed with a bulging arsenal of techniques of quantitative analysis, and of a power – as compared to untrained common sense – comparable to the displacement of archery by cannon. (. . .) It is a scientific revolution of the first magnitude (. . .) I am convinced that economics is finally at the threshold of its golden age (. . .).' See on this Backhouse (1997) and Morgan (2003).

The field of psychology has, in the last 50 years, also turned from a theoretical discipline into an empirical one, with a stronger association with the natural sciences. The well-known Dutch psychologist Hans Crombag (2006) illustrates how the study of psychology dealt with the psyche until well into the 1960s and was more about studying emotions than about hard facts. A human's personality was supposed to consist of several layers of depth (the *Schichtentheorie* or strata theory), including the *Lebensgrund* (existence-related drives), *endothymer Grund* (endothymic ground) and *personeller Oberbau*. The aim was to find the location of emotions in each of these layers, a type of research that took place by having people fill in questionnaires. The revolution came with the behaviourism of B.F. Skinner: the only thing to be trusted is the observable and anything that people say about their motives must be distrusted.

Both in economics and in psychology this shift led to a situation in which the object of study is more and more limited to things that can be modelled (as in economics) or for which empirical proof can be provided (as in psychology). Research that did not make use of these methods became less prestigious in the view of the majority. See Ash (2003, 260) and Porter (1995, 17): 'Among psychologists, it is the weaker students who specialize in the more humane branches: those with lower seconds (. . .).'

I mention the examples of economics and psychology because it would be a rather unattractive prospect if legal science were to develop in the same direction. Legal scholarship should vehemently avoid emulating the methods of these other disciplines. Following in their footsteps can only lead to a situation in which the battle with the other disciplines is lost. Instead, the legal discipline should focus on its strengths. This is where the empirical sciences are weak, namely in reflecting on what people should do as a matter of law in our society and in offering a method to determine this. Clifford Geertz generalizes this point in the following way: 'The quests for general, abstract, situationally unconditioned theory, for precise predictability, and for universally applicable, "objectivist" method are misplaced in research designed to discover why it is that human beings think, feel, and act as they do. To discover how we learn, how we relate to one another, how we understand what happens to us, demands something more, or something other, than the size-up-and-solve mentality of the soi-disant "hard sciences".'

Geertz (2001). See also Porter (1995, 5): quantification 'simply evades the deep and important issues' and makes the discipline poorer than it was before. The plea of Bent Flyvbjerg for a turn in the social sciences is repeated here for the legal discipline. Flyvbjerg (2001) emphasizes that scientists will most certainly lose the debate about the importance of their discipline if they are led by the model of the natural sciences. They should underline instead what is their unique contribution to knowledge about humans; see also *supra*, no. 44. This is also an important public debate: in the German *Frankfurter Allgemeine Zeitung* of 14 June 2009, 83 professors of economics published a cry of distress that university chairs for economics are increasingly occupied by econometricians and mathematical economists without much interest in questions of policy relevant to the German or European economy. In response, 188 other university academics riposted and claimed that the first group apparently wanted to embark upon a German *Sonderweg* in the very international discipline of economics, and sacrifice academic excellence for policy-oriented work.

Deirdre McKloskey (1983) points out that, although economists formally pay lip service to the use of hard methods, they do in the end make use of more traditional argumentative techniques. The knowledge that is obtained from the more prestigious methods does not suffice to answer many of the relevant questions.

It may be important to emphasize that I am also a proponent of using empirical methods in legal scholarship to a greater extent than is the case at present: this will lead to stimulating and creative research. However, this type of work is particularly useful when trying to answer a certain type of questions within the legal discipline. I argue strongly against the notion that knowledge acquired by making use of empirical methods is more trustworthy, or simply better, than insights provided by more traditional methods of research.

> It is problematic that some academics – in particular those practising the empirical sciences – regard only one method (that is to say their own) as a universal panacea. Thus, the famous American biologist, Edward O. Wilson (1998), claims that the existing rift between the natural sciences, on the one hand, and the humanities and social sciences, on the other, must be bridged sooner rather than later. However, in the synthesis he proposes, the methods of the natural sciences (directed towards physical perception) are dominant. See, for criticism of Wilson's reductionist view of the unity of knowledge, Stephen Jay Gould (2003). It is surprising to find that, more than 250 years after Hume's statement (1748 [1975, 165]) about knowledge – 'Does it contain any abstract reasoning concerning quantity or number? No. Does it contain any experimental reasoning concerning matter of fact and existence? No. Commit it then to the flames: for it can contain nothing but sophistry and illusion' – this reductionism is still so influential. It seems safe to conclude that pushing the idea of empirical methods as offering the only 'real' knowledge has proven to be a highly successful strategy in the fight for money and prestige. This can also explain why natural scientists are usually over-represented in awarding prestigious national research prizes (such as the German Leibniz Prize and the Dutch Spinoza Prize).

4. THE RESEARCH CULTURE IN LEGAL ACADEMIA

58. Introduction

This section examines the research culture in legal academia, which is a topic that is just as important for a fertile legal discourse as the requirements that research must be innovative (Section 2) and explicit about its aim and methodology (Section 3). The concern here is to organize research (and teaching) in such a way that it is conducive to the needs of the academic community. This concern determines which perspective is adopted: it is not how to make research as 'manageable' and controllable as possible for policymakers, but how to design the university in such a way that it satisfies the needs of academics themselves. To this end, attention is successively paid in this section to research programmes (no. 59), to the importance of fundamental research, and to the question whether today's market-driven forces curtail these aims (no. 60). This is followed by a sketch of an alternative approach or at least its contours (no. 61). The final section is devoted to legal education (no. 62).

Some readers will possibly consider what follows as striving for a hopelessly old-fashioned and romantic ideal of research and teaching. Perhaps forty years ago, it would have even been considered a cliché. However, I am of the opinion that it would be good to re-establish a number of the old ideals in doing academic work – although not as old as it might seem, namely developed in the beginning of the nineteenth century by Alexander Von Humboldt. This is certainly not a plea for a return to past times, but it is a call for a re-evaluation of some essential university values that have come dangerously close to being overlooked, much to the peril of the universities themselves. I am not alone in expressing this concern: see, in general, Brown (2011) and, more specifically, Dilger (2011) for Germany, Van Oostrom (2007) and Lorenz (2008) for the Netherlands, and Bok (2004) for the United States.

59. Research Programmes

Law was defined in Chapter III as the discipline of conflicting arguments about what ought to be. This view not only leads to the substantive consequences for the character of law that have already been described, but it also means something for the way in which universities should organize their research. The argumentative character of legal science makes it able to profit from debate. Moreover, the emphasis on the importance of creativity (see *supra*, no. 50) means that university policy makers have to stimulate this to the greatest extent possible. Finally, an important task of universities is to train new researchers. In my view, debate, creativity and training are best stimulated by organizing research in the form of research groups that carry out a joint 'research programme'. Each of these aspects is discussed below.

> Research can be organized in different ways. The standard method in many fields throughout the world is to establish coherent sets of research activities having a common mission and tasking groups of people who generally work together on a daily basis to carry out these activities. The phenomenon comes from natural sciences, where group work became necessary for financial and practical reasons, and it was no longer possible to carry out experiments on an individual basis. This was (and still is) particularly true where expensive infrastructure is needed, as exemplified by the European 'Very Large Telescope' (VLT) in Chile or the Large Hadron Collider of CERN in Geneva, involving 7000 researchers from 80 countries.
>
> Organizing legal research by way of programmes has also become the standard in various European countries. Thus, in the Netherlands, almost all research carried out at universities is categorized under programmes at the level of departments, institutes, faculties or (often inter-faculty) research schools. In the last national research assessment in 2009, 59 different programmes in law were evaluated. And even though many of these programmes were originally set up as a result of external pressure (research programming in the Netherlands is often seen as necessary to obtain funding), there are good substantive reasons why like-minded researchers should work together.

The first advantage of working within a research group is that it stimulates academic discussion. Necessary components to fostering a good research culture are an environment where people can freely express ideas, are contradicted by others, are inspired by their colleagues' work and can thus enhance the quality of their own work by way of debate. The American sociologist Robert K. Merton spoke of this as a 'serendipitous microenvironment'. The creation of such a stimulating research culture is an essential responsibility of any university.

See Merton & Barber (2006, 262). Legal science traditionally has an individualist research tradition, but this has taken a turn for the better in the last decade or so. The idea that the quality of research is improved if it is done within 'a community of gifted people working intimately but independently, with each free to follow his own mind' (thus, James B. Fisk, former President of Bell Labs: Shapin 2008, 190) is by now widely accepted: scholars are expected to draw out objections to their drafts and to comment themselves on the drafts of colleagues. This form of informal peer review is perhaps the most important form of quality control one can think of.

The inspiration one can draw from the group is of course strongly dependent on its design. As the Dutch physicist, Ad Lagendijk (1997) has written: 'A professor, a single postdoc and a few PhD-researchers that I see on a daily basis (. . .). Terrific research can thrive in a small group apart from the rest.' Interdisciplinary research can be promoted by encouraging representatives of different disciplines to work together in one group. This is by no means an easy task and the results may lead only to multi-disciplinary insights, meaning that a given problem is approached from different angles without any further integration. Another worthwhile issue for drawing inspiration is the location of meetings. The participants in these groups will surely require access to books and journals, preferably located in open stacks. Having a central location in a common room, where there is a constant stream of visitors could be beneficial to the group as well (cf. infra, no. 56). The Leiden-based Lorentz Centre (for astronomy, mathematics and physics) is in this respect an inspiring example.

Secondly, it must be emphasized that the wider framework of a research group can offer a fertile breeding ground for individual creativity. This may be doubted by those who see research programmes only as an obstacle to good legal research because they believe that real advances are always made by individuals. However, any good research group does not curtail creativity, but stimulates it. This objection drills us in what must be the purpose of research programming: to facilitate an individual researcher's quest for understanding a theme he is fascinated by, and not a straitjacket allowing only a certain type of work.

Ipsen (2005, 427), for example, is critical of research programming and of cooperation among researchers: 'Wesentliche Fortschritte im rechtswissenschaftlichen Diskurs werden (. . .) durch Monographien erzielt.' ('Real progress in legal discourse is made through monographs.') I largely agree but do not see a contradiction here: cooperation should not stand in the way of individual fervour. However, it is safe to say that individual researchers will remain the driving force in pushing legal science forward.

To be fair, in addressing this criticism of research programmes, I will concede, based on my own experiences, that programming sometimes can be restrictive. This is primarily caused by the interest of the research director or programme leader in presenting a coherent output to assessment committees – thus stimulating colleagues to publish as much as possible within the narrow boundaries of the programme. This is why, in my view, assessment committees should attach less importance to the programme description (the 'plans') and more to the realized publications, which should of course still give evidence of some coherence. This argues for brief programme descriptions indicating the field of research, the methods to be used and the type of publication aimed at, without curtailing individual creativity.

An alternative, is not to assess research programmes by themselves, but to assess the output of the faculty as a whole, based on the individual publications of its members. The often-heard objection that this would be logistically impossible is belied by the experience in the United Kingdom, where the Research Assessment Exercise has been organized in this way since 1992 (cf. <www.rae.ac.uk>). This does more justice to the reality that the quality of legal research is ultimately dependent on individual achievements. To assume that assessing a programme would say anything about the quality of its individual members presupposes a different type of exercise of scholarly activities than is usually the case in legal science. At American law schools research programmes are almost entirely absent.

Thirdly, a research group offers the ideal environment for young (PhD) researchers, where they are trained and looked after by their senior colleagues and can share their experiences with other young colleagues.

Several European countries have in the last decade set up 'graduate schools' for their PhD researchers (unlike the American model, these schools do not include master students). Graduate schools (either at the university or faculty level) usually offer courses and carry formal responsibility for the well-being of the doctoral students. They potentially have the big advantage that they can fight parochialism by bringing together researchers from different fields. In the Netherlands, several law faculties have chosen a different model: they work together in so-called 'research schools', sometimes even having common research programmes of three or four different law faculties. In particular the Ius Commune Research School (<www.iuscommune.eu>), which was founded in 1995, has proved to be successful: it unites a large part of the PhD researchers and senior staff members in the Netherlands who work in the fields of European private law, European constitutional law, and comparative law. However, more important than these large networks, is the micro-climate of the direct working environment (see above).

60. The Market and the Importance of Fundamental Research

Yet another essential aspect of the research culture in legal academia is that the culture is supposed to stimulate creative and fundamental research. The responsibility of the university does not primarily lie with offering services to society or with doing research that is of immediate relevance to the general public, but with a search for fundamental knowledge. Although this Humboldtian ideal is widely accepted by universities and funding organizations throughout the world, it is under threat – as it has always been.

> The primary motivation of any academic researcher must be his personal passion for doing scholarly work. This means that the university should cherish the individuality and headstrong character of the good researcher: innovation always comes from the margins and what counts in the end is the academic output. Gifted academics must therefore be able to pursue their own research agenda. This is also the case because it is difficult to say in advance what is the best thing to do to make progress (cf. Vranken 2006, 30).
>
> It is therefore highly positive that funding organizations increasingly grant money on the basis of individual merit. This can be seen in the personal prizes created by national funding organizations (such as the German Leibniz Prize and the Dutch Spinoza Prize as well as Innovational Research Incentives Schemes), but also in the Starting grants and Advanced grants established by the European Research Council in 2007. However, it takes more than this to foster a research culture with a focus on stimulating creativity. Here, one can make great progress by taking small steps. Thus, the culture of (international) academic prizes for legal research is relatively undeveloped. Mathematics and economics each have their own prize for the best researcher under forty, namely the Fields Medal (awarded since 1936) and the John Bates Clark Medal (established in 1947). These examples are worth following. Individual law faculties can also create prize contests for advanced students (which also happens to be an excellent way to recruit PhD-researchers). This is in line with the largely accepted insight that these types of symbolic rewards are better at enhancing intrinsic motivation than financial incentives (cf. Osterloh & Frey 2010 and *infra*).

The biggest threat to fundamental and creative research is the strong increase in market efficiency at universities. This phenomenon can be observed in many countries. At its core, is the creation of an atmosphere of distrust towards academics, and a belief in control and accountability to guarantee a higher quality of research. This is why a group of prestigious

European universities recently sounded the tocsin about this development and made a plea for valuing precisely those elements of academic research that are not manageable, such as creativity and serendipity. Their warning is against the fallacy of management in removing things if they cannot be managed or they make management more difficult.

> This call (Boulton & Lucas 2008) was made by the League of European Research Universities (LERU) that includes, for example, the universities of Oxford, Cambridge, Munich, Helsinki and Leiden. Their challenge to market-driven targets that turn universities into providers of valorized knowledge and jeopardize their fundamental mission is mirrored in the pleas made by prominent academics, including the former President of Harvard University, Derek Bok (2004), and the former President of the Royal Netherlands Academy of Arts and Sciences, Frits van Oostrom (2006). They both warn of a climate in which to 'score' in the short term is sometimes seen as being more important than to do fundamental and curiosity-driven research. Van Oostrom describes how departments increasingly function as counters for all kinds of subsidies caused by the lack of backbone in academics and their administrators. The theme is further explored by Pels (2003), Lorenz (2008) – under the illuminating title, *If you're So Smart, Why aren't you Rich?* – and Regini (2011).

The basis for reducing universities to organizations driven by market efficiency originated in the principles of the new public management, particularly based on the idea that competition among individuals or research groups will lead to higher quality outputs. The underlying premise in this model is that quality can be measured by way of so-called 'performance indicators'. The positive thing about this is that the emphasis lies on the performance: no matter what the previously formulated plans were or how much time was invested, the quality of academic publications is all that matters in the end. In this regard, market thinking is a proper form of debureaucratization and can offer an incentive to perform well. However, this overlooks the perverse effects of performance measurement. There are, in particular, two such effects that make the application of market efficiency to fundamental and creative academic research (and education) problematic.

> There is an abundance of literature on the new public management (the application of management techniques developed for business to the public sector). Although performance measurement furthers transparency, efficiency, and accountability, its disadvantages are also widely recognized: in addition to the two drawbacks discussed below, it is well known that they are likely to advance strategic behaviour (those being measured learn how to manipulate the indicators), do not stimulate innovation (reproduction of previous work will often lead to a higher score) and can lead to a tunnel vision ('targetitis'). See Thiel & Leeuw (2002), De Bruijn (2002) and the contributions to Lorenz (2008).

The first negative effect of the use of performance measurement is that it is only directed at the measurable aspects of performance, such as the number of publications or citations, the type of journal an article was published in, or whether a clear research question was formulated in the first few pages of the publication. This means that even if one is able to formulate clear tools for measurement of legal research – which is not so likely in the varied legal discipline – they will not be able to include all aspects of quality. In other words, the intangibles, or what cannot be counted by measurement, simply become irrelevant. This can lead to perverse incentives for those academics who greatly value performance measurement. In a quest for prestige and tenure they might be tempted to trade in their professional *habitus* for an urge to score highly and deliver as many measurable achievements as possible. However, it is likely that researchers valued more highly by the community of scholars are not motivated by performing in the short term, and will be motivated by something else, namely by their quest for knowledge. This means that performance measurement does not say everything about the quality of the completed research, which always requires a substantive judgement by peers.

Research shows that introduction of performance measurement often leads to the neglect of long-term goals: an organization that scores highly today on the measurable factors is likely to score badly in the long run because of its neglect of the non-measurable factors that are important in increasing innovation and employee satisfaction. See De Bruijn (2002). This carries a risk of perverse effects: it is certain that researchers have to be productive, but publishing twenty articles a year does not in itself make someone a better researcher. It is more likely that, in this case, a slicing strategy was applied: research was divided over as many papers as possible as if it were a sausage. The better thing to do would have been to make one lengthy article or book that is likely to have a bigger impact in the long term. For the same reason one can criticize a unilateral focus on counting PhD defences as a quality indicator: performance measurement in general tells us surprisingly little about true quality. The adverse effects of performance indicators have also been identified in healthcare: the quantitative measuring of achievements does not enhance the quality of hospitals or family doctors, but tends to reduce intrinsic motivation to do the right thing, see for example Bevan & Hood (2006).

This discussion makes it clear that the principal function of performance indicators is to make partly explicit what we can expect a researcher to do (see also *infra*, no. 61). It also shows that rewarding researchers based on quantitative criteria does not necessarily lead to a higher quality of work. Any academic worth his salt is driven by something else, that is to say what Shapin 2008, 263 calls 'the desire for a "free space" in which to conduct the inquiries that one wants to conduct, that one might even feel oneself driven to conduct'. Such an animated and single-minded researcher will lose his motivation if his work disintegrates in a business-like fashion into quantifiable factors of measurement. Because he is not trusted as an academic, he degenerates from a passionate professional into an externally directed anonymous 'processor'. This is a well-known phenomenon in other fields as well: job motivation diminishes as soon as quality is only measured in terms of quantitative output. See Lorenz (2008, 179), and Osterloh & Frey (2010, 14): 'Autonomy is the most important precondition for intrinsic motivation, which in turn is required for creative research.'

Secondly, market thinking – if taken seriously – leads to a form of competition that is wrong for the university. Academic practice is already as competitive as can be: each researcher strives to write the most thought-provoking books and articles and to teach students in the best possible way. The achievements of colleagues in this respect are a permanent source of comparison and inspiration. In addition to this, the academic community as a forum of judgement decides how research is to be valued: first with the acceptance of the manuscript by the editorial board of the journal or book series, and then, after the actual publication, by all other peers. In addition, active academics are perpetually assessed in other ways: through grant applications: consideration for editorial boards: invitations to conference lectures: and so on). Competition in this sense is inherent in academic life.

However, this type of competition is fundamentally different from the sort that is propagated under the new public management. Thus, the Leiden Professor of Astrophysics, Vincent Icke, warns that competition along the lines of the business model leads to the formation of *blocs*, chauvinism and short-term thinking, all of which are counterproductive to science. As discussed above, Frits van Oostrom warns against the dangers of organizing a faculty into a federative whole in which the separate sections – indeed as if they were business units – have to fight for their own profit, and cooperation with colleagues next door is seen as betrayal.

See Icke (in Lorenz 2008, 256) and Van Oostrom (2007, 14). In terms of the new public management, this means that financial competition drives out the so-called 'system responsibility': because units are supposed to compete with each other, they no longer work together and do not share their knowledge. The lack of openness, discussion and cooperation caused by this is at odds with the type of competition that science is all about: not for the money, but for the appeal of ideas, and therefore – as Bourdieu (1984) claims – for symbolic capital in the form of reputation. This competition is as strong in little fields as in international scholarship. Icke (in Lorenz 2008, 257) rightly describes it as being of a staggering fierceness: 'An academic telling nonsense in a lecture or at a colloquium or conference is not mildly censured, but torn to shreds.' It has already been seen above (no. 50) that publishing insights that go against prevailing opinion is sometimes met with heavy resistance. It is also unproven that economic competition leads to better research. This belief was manifest in the action of Rainer Goebel, a well-known German professor of Neurocognition, who repeatedly declined offers to exchange Maastricht for Stanford, claiming that doing so would force him to compete with his colleagues rather than collaborate with them.

61. An Alternative Approach

The previous section described the consequences of market thinking on (fundamental) academic research and education. These consequences have luckily not materialized yet. For example, the extent to which performance measurement is seen as important is, in the end, dependent on the administrator's desire to be in control. In the law faculties, this administrator is, in most cases, someone who is a legal scholar himself and therefore aware of the limited value of performance indicators. And yet, there is every reason to sketch the contours of how things could be done differently. This section will make three main points regarding this alternative approach.

An alternative approach is also needed because European law faculties are highly dependent on the central university administration, which is in turn dependent on government funding. There can come a moment when the external administrative pressures become so acute that law faculties have to swallow new public management techniques in governing their organization. The worst case scenario here, and what the universities must prevent at all costs, is for the assessment of performance indicators to fall in the hands of a micro-managing macho manager, which would surely lead to the perversion of the system already discussed, turning assessments into bureaucratic, pointless rituals. Cf. De Bruijn (2002).

First, it must be emphasized that there is nothing wrong with developing performance indicators in and of itself because they do in fact clarify what the university can expect from its academics. However, it is essential that these indicators are not purely based on quantitative factors, but are also suited to measuring quality: they must reflect what the academic community sees as good legal research. And even if this requirement is met, it must be accepted that they can only be used as instruments in a broader context, and can never be considered as valid replacements for peer evaluations. Furthermore, they should have only a limited role when it comes to determining funding.

The literature is unanimous in saying that performance indicators must only be used moderately. See, amongst many others, De Bruijn (2002) and Thiel & Leeuw (2002). This is reflected in reports on the value of research assessments issued by various agencies dealing with higher education. Thus, in the European Commission's report, *Assessing Europe's University-Based Research* (2010, 36ff.), it is argued that 'those being assessed need to have confidence that the indicators are appropriate and truthful'. In the Netherlands, the various reports published by the Association of Universities in the Netherlands (VSNU 2005 and 2007) and the Royal Netherlands Academy of Arts and Sciences (KNAW 2005 and 2011) say the same thing. This makes it important that legal science does not yield to the temptation of developing indicators that are comparable to those in other disciplines (such as citation analysis and elaborate rankings of journals) if the use of these methods does not lead to a fair judgement of what legal scholars regard as good research. This is why these reports do not primarily look at measurable factors, but at qualitative indicators instead (such as the substantive quality of publications and so-called 'esteem indicators' that reflect how the research community regards an individual researcher – based on awards, fellowships, keynote addresses, editorial roles, organization of conferences and elected memberships of academies). In addition to this, the reports emphasize that research assessments must always pay attention to the 'story' behind the numbers (see also De Bruijn 2002) and that administrators should accept that not everything can be quantified. Put differently, there must be some resistance, at least, to the natural inclination of managers to make research as measurable as possible.

There is a recent tendency to give a large role to bibliometric factors in reaching a judgement about the quality of legal research. It is certainly not impossible to make use of these factors in law and humanities, but – as emphasized in a recent report issued by the KNAW (2011, 43) – 'bibliometric quality indicators must be used cautiously. Counting articles measures only productivity; counting citations measures impact, which is not necessarily the same thing as quality (. . .).' Fifty journals in the field of humanities therefore recently indicated they no longer wished to be classified in the European Reference Index for the Humanities, not because they ranked low in this index (which was not the case), but because of their view that this ranking 'depends on a fundamental misunderstanding of conduct and publication of research in our field, and in the humanities in general. (. . .) Great research may be published anywhere and in any language. Truly ground-breaking work may be more likely to appear from marginal, dissident or unexpected sources, rather than from a well-established and entrenched mainstream. Our journals are various, heterogeneous and distinct. Some are aimed at a broad, general and international readership, others are more specialized in their content and implied audience. Their scope and readership say nothing about the quality of their intellectual content' (Cook et al. 2009).

In order to avoid simplistic judgements based on bibliometric factors alone, one must also be careful about the introduction of a 'points system' in measuring quality. Such systems can be useful, but they overplay their part if they refer to other criteria for quality than those accepted by the academic community. Siems (2008, 148) cites Ruhl, who has proposed to introduce a scale of points to rank academic work in law. His suggestion is to give two points to descriptive doctrinal work and ten points to empirical work, if this studies the influence of law on society. Another example of a points system and its application can be seen in a ranking of German law faculties (see Ipsen 2005, 426) using the number of pages (three or four pages: one point; more than 100 pages: fifteen points) and the status of the journal (if

> peer reviewed, the score was to be multiplied by a factor three) as variables. Ipsen rightly qualifies this system as 'hostile to books' because the academic legal forum does not consider books as inherently inferior to articles. This is confirmed if one carries out citation analyses of law journals: these usually show that books are the most-cited sources. A specific analysis of the 2005 volume of the Dutch main journal for private law (*Nederlands Tijdschrift voor Burgerlijk Recht*) shows that of the 1089 references in total, 547 are to books and contributions to books (the most cited journal being that journal itself).
>
> Another consequence of the limited value of performance indicators is that we must be careful about transferring money from so-called 'internal funding' (mostly government funding) to 'external funding' (such as funding by research councils and charities). This is so not only because the government takes money away from universities and tasks funding organizations to redistribute it (which is a good thing if based on quality assessment), but also because universities themselves make the distribution of money between faculties increasingly contingent on the faculties' external funding sources and their ability to attract commercial funding from private companies. This is denounced by many, including Van Oostrom (2006), who labelled this as an attack on the academic heart of the university: money for fundamental research and for new PhD positions must now increasingly be obtained through funding organizations, even though there is no evidence that doing so will lead to a better qualitative output. It seems obnoxious to have to fight for every penny in order to be able to do what the university is for.

This leads me to the second point. Ultimately, the assessment of research must always come from colleagues within the academic community (peers). As already indicated above (no. 60), international scholarly practice is full of assessment mechanisms. Peer review is not limited to decisions about publications, but extends also to academic appointments, assessment of research proposals, invitations to conferences, election to editorial boards, and so on. Although this method is certainly not ideal, assessment by colleagues seems to be the best possible option.

The inability of bibliometric methods to measure the quality of legal research accurately is the very reason why the importance of the peer review process must be valued above all else. This is also why the United Kingdom Research Assessment Exercise in 2008 decided to evaluate submissions relying on 'panel J' (dealing with law) on the basis of a detailed examination of virtually all the submitted outputs 'on their own merits'. After careful consideration, it was also decided that the exercise would not rank any of the journals. The importance of peer review is confirmed by the KNAW report, *Judging Research on its Merits* (2005), which concluded that, in any research assessment, the main publications are to be assessed by peers, simply because only colleagues can judge what is the best and what is not.

This does not mean that peer review is ideal, but it does mean that there is nothing better, at least at this current juncture of legal scholarship. The disadvantages are described in detail by Edmond (2008) and in more expressive language by Ad Lagendijk (1998): 'It is often driving me mad. If you scored well six times in a row with your grant applications, it is obvious to assume that the quality is also high the seventh time around. But this could not be further from the truth: the seventh time the complete assessment circus is again let loose on you and you are supposed to fill in all these forms. I know that this is the price one has to pay for being allowed to work with the taxpayer's money.' The fact that peer review by editorial boards does not bring universal happiness either is shown by two well-known cases. In 1996, the prominent journal *Social Text* published an article by the American physicist Alan Sokal. The article was, in the words of Sokal (1996) himself, 'a pastiche of left-wing cant, fawning references, grandiose quotations, and outright nonsense' and he had submitted it only to demonstrate the obliviousness of the editors, who found much more importance in who had written it, and how it sounded, than in actually assessing its contents. Similarly in 2002, a young German physicist, Jan Hendrik Schön made similar exposé of the peer review system, although in his case, his intent was more malicious: in a relatively short time, he managed to have no less than 28 of his articles accepted by prestigious journals such as *Nature*, *Science* and *Physical Review Letters*. Despite the supposedly meticulous review procedure, the great majority of these articles proved to be fraudulent.

The use of peer review implies that colleagues within the academic sub-community have a shared notion of what is ‘good’ research. I can deal briefly with this after everything that I have said above about the importance of creative research and of methodological pluralism: good research is creative and creativity comes in many varieties. This diversity is also fruitful because it allows us to appreciate different approaches and acknowledge that jurists can contribute in their own way to obtaining greater knowledge of the law. It also seems to be the international consensus that one type of research is not in itself better than another.

See *supra*, nos. 51 and 57. It is important to clarify what makes particular research good. There seems to be international unanimity about the requirement that good academic work in law should be original or creative. The British Research Assessment Exercise (RAE) adds that originality, significance and rigour are the three criteria that contribute most to the quality of an article, while in Germany ‘interdisciplinarity’ and ‘internationalization’ are the keywords of good research (Ipsen 2005, 425). Korobkin (1999, 860), on American research, comments, that ‘“valuable” scholarship is that which is both insightful and original’ and Chemerinsky (2009, 891) asks of scholarship that it be significant and original. This is also reflected in the reports of the Dutch VSNU-committees on the quality of legal research (VSNU 2005 and 2007) and in the Flemish approach (<www.vlir.be>).

These general requirements leave much room for further interpretation, and rightly so, as there are many types of research that might meet these requirements. With Siems (2008, 248), I am of the opinion that the only right approach is one of tolerance. This is not any different in other disciplines. As the Fields Medal winner, Terence Tao (2007), who offers a non-exhaustive enumeration of as many as 21 types of ‘good’ mathematical research, claims: ‘this diverse and multifaceted nature of “good mathematics” is very healthy for mathematics as a whole, as it allows us to pursue many different approaches to the subject, and exploit many different types of mathematical talent.’

The assessment mechanisms ingrained in scholarly practice must not be replaced by bibliometric criteria. Instead, an attractive alternative, which could ensure high quality academic work, is the proposal made by Margit Osterloh and Bruno Frey, which promotes a careful selection and socialization of aspiring scholars. In their view, recruitment is the essential element of quality control: future colleagues should master the state of the art, have a 'taste for science' and be able to direct themselves. As soon as someone is appointed on the basis of these assets and other strict professional academic criteria (quality of publications and of teaching), this person should be trusted and be given a wide range of autonomy. It may be that some will misuse their autonomy and waste funds, but this is the price to be paid for the majority of high performers to flourish. Most hired researchers are likely to be motivated by the autonomy and resources they receive. The existence of basic funding for everyone who meets the high standards to be recruited will also guarantee a diversity of different approaches. This is the system of quality control employed at top law schools in the United States, including but not limited to Harvard University and the University of Chicago.

See Osterloh & Frey (2010, 15ff.), who emphasize that continuous research assessments only lead to mediocrity: 'Measurement exerts not only pressure to produce predictable but unexciting research outcomes (. . .). Path-breaking contributions are exactly those at variance with accepted criteria' (cf. Frey & Osterloh 2006, 5). Having to meet identical standards (and hence less methodological pluralism) means that one is no longer able to broaden one's horizon. This is why these authors propose to trade in the distribution of means on the basis of output control for distribution based on process control, with the most important criteria being whether the selection procedures is adequate and whether academics have sufficient autonomy. Differentiation among scholars is possible in the way described by Lagendijk (1997): 'Decide on basis of past performance who are the best academics, give them ample funds for a five-year-period and assess them rigorously afterwards' (see also *supra*, no. 60).

The third point is that administrators and academics must show determination in pursuing what they see as the main mission of their university. Administrators are increasingly prone to argue in favour of the type of research they desire under the guise of enhancing quality. There is nothing against a faculty taking the deliberate decision to (for example) devote itself to international or empirical research, or instead, aim for producing the best future practitioners. However, such choices must not be motivated by claiming that one type of research is intrinsically better than another. Academics, for their part, must not be led astray by the control mechanisms of the new public management and should primarily push their own research agenda. In particular, university chairs have a role as exemplars here.

I am of the opinion that universities should make well-founded choices in favour of certain types of research and education more than they currently do. The overwhelming majority of law faculties in Europe focus on teaching national law. It is also difficult to maintain that there are many differences in substance or quality between most law faculties within a country. When it comes to research, choices are sometimes made but then often obscured with a reference to the supposedly higher quality of a certain type of research (usually the more internationally oriented). Although I openly advocate a much more international education and research agenda (see also *infra*, no. 62), I do not mean to suggest that the quality of a more domestically focused education is necessarily any less than an education with a more international focus.

Academics must also show more courage and argue that their job is first and foremost a creative one that can therefore never be made entirely subject to managerial control. The development that Steven Shapin (2008) describes – from science as a vocation to science as a completely professional career – is luckily not complete. This is because an academic should not be a mere bureaucrat, but a charismatic leader (as Max Weber (1946) famously said). Relying on the witness reports of their students, paradigmatic examples of charismatic academic leaders in the last century include notable figures such as Albert Einstein, Richard Feynman and Johan Huizinga and – in law – Harry Lawson, Otto Kahn-Freund, David Daube and René David. They all spread the word about the importance of their field and propagated – as Feynman (1999) calls it – 'the pleasure of finding things out'.

62. Consequences for Legal Education

The focus of this book until now has been almost exclusively on legal research. It would, however, be wrong to suggest that legal scholarship can stand apart from teaching the law: ideally the two are closely related. This is why this last section of the book pays particular attention to the consequences for legal education of the views discussed above about law and legal research. These consequences flow directly from the argumentative character of law (see in particular nos. 31 and 40 above), Legal education must be as little directed towards finding 'certain' rules or outcomes as legal scholarship. The main aim of legal education must be to explore and contrast the implications of conflicting normative positions. Students should not just learn one system of law, but ought to be exposed to alternative ways of achieving justice. The focus is then on learning a way of thinking, much more than on getting to know the intricate details of some substantive law. The following sections discuss the arguments in favour of this new type of legal education and how it can be enacted.

It is surprising that legal education in Europe is usually focused on presenting the law as coming from some authority and therefore on how it is. Thus, virtually all textbooks aim to give a description of the existing national law, seemingly trying to ban uncertainty as much as possible. This does not only make legal education positivist and national, it also makes it too focused on the contents of the rules, although we know that this tends to change rapidly.

Atiyah & Summers (1987, 394) note the same thing: 'The tone of textbooks is often dogmatic, with decisions presented as if they were strict decisions from basic principles. (. . .) The ultimate and all-pervasive aim is to lay out the law as it stood on the day the book went to press.' This positivist thinking carries the risk that students become obsessed with the here and now without reflecting upon how the law could read. This insight that legal education must not focus on the apparent certainties introduced by the national legislature and courts is of course not new. Rudolf Von Jhering ([1998, 52]) was already writing back in 1868 about positivism as the 'mortal enemy' of jurisprudence: 'it downgrades legal science to a mere trade and must therefore be fought to the death'.

The best legal education ought to teach students a method: they need to learn which arguments exist for and against certain solutions, how to weigh these arguments and how to deal with competing systems of rules. This means that the curriculum must be much more international than it is today: students should learn about the fact that different societies give a different weight to issues such as social justice, efficiency, the equality of men and women, and the value of life. They should learn to think through the consequences of choices made in different societies, to understand why these choices were made, and to argue why they think one choice is better than the other. The starting point, therefore, is not the German or French (or any other national) law, but a particular question and the way in which this question is answered in various jurisdictions. This calls for a truly European (or global) education in the bachelor phase of the curriculum, followed by a masters in one specific national legal system.

Three arguments can be put forward in favour of a more international approach to teaching the law. The first is based on the changing character of the law itself, the second on the requirements an academic study should meet, and the third on the importance of attracting highly motivated students to law programmes. See also Smits (2011).

The first argument in favour of a truly European education is that the law itself is no longer a national phenomenon. The law increasingly flows from sources outside the national border and is often the product of private initiatives (see *supra*, no. 25). Any modern legal education should take these norms into account, not only because they are indispensable in understanding the existing law (and consequently play a big role in practice), but also because they make students realize that the law is not necessarily tied to the nation state. Patrick Glenn (2006, 59) rightly observes that if the law is no longer considered exclusively in terms of national sources, the discipline of law 'must assume the cognitive burden of providing information on law beyond national borders' (also see *supra*, no. 39). This implies that a legal education based exclusively on the intricacies of national legislation and court decisions is an inadequate one.

It would be possible to argue that this plurality of sources does not force us to adopt any far-reaching type of international legal education: one could still teach the national law and add some international and comparative elements here and there. I do not deny this as a possibility (it is even common practice at most law schools), but I do not think that this is the best way to teach students in today's globalizing world. Even if one asserts that the only goal of legal education is to offer a professional training for future practitioners (which I would deny), these practitioners should be able to work in different legal systems in various countries to meet their clients' needs. Even when graduates stay in their home country, they are increasingly advising multinational and foreign clients who want to know about different solutions. This calls for a much more rigorous international curriculum in which alternative approaches are sketched from the first day. Thus, teaching only one national law does not adequately prepare students for the world they have to work in.

In the last decade, the attention given to comparative and European aspects of the law has increased significantly in most curricula. Various international joint degree programmes were put into place, including the Dutch-German Hanse Law School. Recent overviews of this development can be found in special issues on transnational legal education in the *Penn State International Law Review* (26 (2008) no. 4) and in the *German Law Journal* (10 (2009) no. 7). The premise of these curricula is that one must first learn the 'own' (national) law and that only in the second stage can attention be paid to foreign law. The stimulating experiences of the Maastricht European Law School and the 'transsystemic' curriculum of the McGill Faculty of Law in Montreal (where from the very first year, civil law and common law are taught in an integrated way) show that this can be done differently. I have no doubt that this integrative model is the best teaching method available to meet the needs of an international legal education. Students dealing with problems that require considerations of multiple jurisdictions tend to form pluralistic legal minds contrary to the 'mind fixing' that takes place under the traditional curriculum. As Jaakko Husa (2009) rightly says: 'This creates an implicit mono-epistemology, which makes lawyers regard their own system as "normal" and other systems as "not-normal" or, at least, something that is "less-normal". From this mono-epistemic platform, the law student is first immersed in the one-approach-thinking, which later makes it difficult to epistemologically adapt to transnational pluralism and to genuinely accept different approaches.'

The rise of these new types of transnational curricula was characterized as a new 'Langdellian moment' (Strauss 2006). In the same way as Christopher Columbus Langdell initiated a reform of American legal education towards the end of the nineteenth century by introducing the Socratic method, McGill and Maastricht lead the way towards a more international legal education. This is not without difficulties: this integrated method requires not only new teaching materials and the hiring of staff members with international experience, but it also implies that graduates may not have direct access to the legal profession because the legislation has yet to adapt to the needs of a rapidly internationalizing society. If these problems can be overcome, it will lead to truly international law faculties that will be able to compete for students and staff from all over Europe. In addition, it will lead to a much-desired differentiation among law faculties (see also *supra*, no. 61).

The second argument in favour of an international legal education is that it meets the requirements of an academic study better (on these requirements: Bell 2003 and Kronman 2007). A legal education should, in my view, do at least two things: it should offer a specialized professional training in becoming a lawyer and it should shape students to become academics. The latter means that students should learn to use the law not only as an instrument, but also to think about it in an intellectual way. Martha Nussbaum (2003) aptly argues that in today's world, this academic aspect means that students have to prepare for 'global citizenship': they should learn how to become a citizen, not only of their country and their local community, but also of the increasingly interlocking and interdependent world that they live in. This means, in my view, that an academic legal education should educate students about the contingency of the law: students have to be exposed to legal diversity, not only through grasping common law and civil law (and the varieties within these legal families), but also by extending their understanding to Nordic, Asian and Islamic laws. These jurisdictions will tell them how different choices can be made. If this 'dialogue with otherness' (cf. Morisette 2002) is at the core of legal education, to focus on only one or two jurisdictions would be a poor and rather limited curriculum. A true legal education is only worth its salt if it shows alternative outcomes to common problems to the full extent.

It must be emphasized that this argument is not just about teaching students about multiple legal systems; it is about encouraging students to learn the legal way of thinking (to 'think like a lawyer'). It is similar in a way to what economists do in adopting a method of analysis ('the economic approach'): law is ideally regarded as a method and not as a subject. Under this view, students no longer study English law or German law, but they learn how to apply a legal approach to the questions that society is facing. In doing so, they learn that views on 'what ought to be' necessarily differ from one jurisdiction to another, and that legal scholarship deals with exploring and contrasting the implications of these conflicting normative positions. Legal scholars do not search for what the just society is, but discuss alternatives. Although after two hundred years of teaching only one law, many law schools may be apprehensive of, or even resistant to, such a transition, it does not mean that it is impossible. One should realize that in the 1000 years or so in which the law has been taught at universities, the last two hundred years have been exceptional: before the dawn of the nineteenth century, students learned about more than one law, be it Roman law and canon law, common law and mercantile law, or Roman law and local law. It was self-evident that all of these laws had a rationality of their own and could not be brought under one heading. The academic degrees that law graduates receive (LL.B (*legum baccalaureus* or Bachelor of Laws), LL.M (*legum magister* or Master of Laws) and LL.D (Doctor of Laws) still remind us of this practice.

The final argument for why an international legal education is preferable to a national one is that it will attract students who are more motivated. In this respect, the success story of the curriculum reform made by Langdell at Harvard is telling: before Langdell became the dean of Harvard Law School in 1870, law was taught by way of lectures, textbooks and moot courts. This was good enough for the great majority of students, but it did not give any real intellectual stimulation to the best among them. This all changed when Langdell introduced the case method (and combined it with the Socratic method). This new method significantly intensified the academic rigour of the programme, which in turn attracted more ambitious students, craving intellectual stimulation, to the programme. After graduation, these students were hired by the top law firms in New York because of their ability to deal with more than one state's jurisdiction (Strauss 2006). In most European countries today, the pursuit of a legal education is seen as a rather meek pursuit. This is at least partly caused by the way in which law is often taught, portrayed as something authoritative and inalterable. I believe this perception of the law is wrong. A European or cosmopolitan legal education can be a real intellectual challenge, attracting even more capable students and producing better graduates.

Furthermore, international legal education need not take place in the language of the country where the university is located: an international law curriculum can be taught in English (or in any other language). The objections sometimes expressed against teaching law in English stem generally from the fear that in learning about non-English legal concepts in English, a certain essence of those concepts might get lost in the translation. However, a valid reason to quash these fears is to realize that the emphasis of European or global legal education is not on what the actual texts say or their interpretation, but on the arguments behind the concepts.

Of course, it does not make any sense (nor should one try) to teach Dutch, German, Finnish, or another national law, in English. However, this is not the point of the type of European legal education proposed in this section: the aim of such a programme would be teach students to think like a lawyer in an international setting. This means a necessary turn away from the texts and their interpretation towards the arguments behind these texts. These arguments can very well be discussed in English as they are not dependent on one national jurisdiction. The prerequisite is that international textbooks in English become available on a much larger scale than is the case today. See, on English as a language for *research*, also *supra*, no. 48.

Another point of discussion is what the most effective model of teaching is in a transnational legal curriculum. If we assume that students are to be persuaded to consider a wide variety of sources to construct their own understanding (and not that of the learned author or lecturer) of the legal problem, the ideal teaching method is certainly not to focus on doctrinal questions or to teach 'comparative law' as such. What works best is to select a topic and to provide materials on how this topic is dealt with in various jurisdictions.

Kurt Lipstein (1992, 258) aptly describes the ideal process: 'The student must in his time examine the reading matter, possibly have recourse to further literature and practice cited there before coming to the classroom. Here accounts given by members of the class reporting on unfamiliar topics will be amplified, collected and explained by the lecturer (. . .). This exchange (. . .) requires a much greater participation by the directing lecturer and the audience (. . .).' This practice fits in with various 'teaching theories'. One of these theories is problem-based learning (PBL), adopted at various law schools throughout the world including Maastricht University's Faculty of Law (see, on this faculty's European Law School programme, Heringa & Akkermans 2011). PBL regards discussion of carefully designed problems in small groups, rather than systematic overviews in big lectures, as the main stimulus for learning. PBL can work well if it is sufficiently adapted to legal education and understood in a broad sense as focusing on a discussion of problems with multiple solutions. In my own experience, a vital component of successful PBL is the lecturer's qualification as a reputable academic rather than as a mere 'facilitator' of discussions. As George Stigler (1963, 14) once put it: he is 'to fan the spark of genuine intellectual curiosity and (. . .) to communicate the enormous adventure and the knightly conduct in the quest for knowledge'.

PBL is not the only educational theory consistent with small group teaching aimed at an exchange of ideas about alternative problem solving. The Socratic method, consisting of a dialogue between lecturer and students, in question and answer format, also enables 'deep' learning. In American law schools, this Socratic method is seen as a highly successful approach to two things PBL also does: teach students to think like a lawyer and to practise their skills. I do not think PBL and the Socratic method differ fundamentally, except for the fact that in PBL, there seems to be a preference for smaller groups of students with twelve being about the maximum. However, the American experience shows it is very possible to teach larger groups of students. See also Rakoff & Minow (2007).

Synopsis

63. Four Claims

This book began with the observation that the aims, methods and organization of legal scholarship have received a lot of attention in the last few years. What followed can be seen as an attempt to cope with this 'identity crisis'. This synopsis does not offer a detailed summary of that attempt but, instead, highlights four key points, which in my view are essential if we are to take legal scholarship seriously and avert the crisis that confronts legal scholars.

First, a clearer vision of the tasks assigned to legal scholarship is required. Legal academics can pursue different goals but, in my view, the core of their discipline is the question, 'What are people legally obliged to do?' The accompanying research method is to identify and to think through arguments for and against certain solutions and to see whether these arguments can be accepted or not in the normative setting of a specific jurisdiction. Existing jurisdictions are thus seen as 'laboratories' in dealing with conflicting normative positions. One need not accept this specific interpretation of the task of legal science to recognize that a clearer formulation of its aim is needed. The legal discipline will otherwise remain a pariah in the company of other academic disciplines that can describe precisely what is at their core.

Secondly, this interpretation puts it beyond doubt that legal science cannot simply rely on the authority of the legislature and the judiciary to answer the question, 'What ought we legally to do?' Those in power have always claimed that the law is given by an authority and, hence, is no more suited to further discussion than God giving the Ten Commandments to Moses, the Oracle at Delphi giving Lycurgus the laws of Sparta, or Napoleon dispensing the Code Civil. Jurists know better than this. The core of the academic engagement with the law (at least in the normative sense) is to show time and time again how we can debate what ought to be, even if there is already a consensus amongst the majority. The theoretical foundation of this was a view of the law as an organically growing whole, 'fined and refined by an infinite number of grave and learned men' (as the student says in Hobbes's *A Dialogue between a Philosopher and a Student of the Common Laws of England*).

A third claim made in this book is that legal scholarship offers, most of all, a way of thinking: while the contents of the positive law are changeable, the legal academic must aim for the development of a method that can deal with the available materials. Again, the proposed 'empirical-normative' method need not be accepted as the only right one, as long as it is acknowledged that it is only by defining legal scholarship as a way of thinking, that it will no longer be dependent on the coincidental contents of the positive law. Inevitably, this also turns law into an international discipline and, that being the case, to make use of only national materials in answering the question, 'What ought we legally to do?', becomes blatantly inadequate.

The final claim is that, if anything, legal scholarship must be original and in order to foster and nurture creativity, a research culture that allows freedom to the gifted researcher must be promoted. If too strictly enforced, 'market thinking' with a unilateral focus on the measurability of performance would only obstruct the free flow of ideas and hinder creativity and motivation. It is also of great importance for law faculties to realize and understand that quality can come in many varieties. Restricting the types of research and teaching to a single 'best' method, is not likely to guarantee a high quality product.

All in all, this book provides the insight that the legal discipline must not be heavily influenced by the aims and methods

of other disciplines, which are often limited to understanding the social or physical reality. What the legal discipline must do instead is to capitalize on its strength, which is its ability to reflect upon what people and organizations legally ought to do.

References

The references used in this book are to the author and the year of first publication. Letters were added in case of reference to more publications of the same author in the same year (2008a, 2008b, etc.).

Ankersmit, F.R. (2001), *Historical Representation*, Stanford: Stanford University Press

Aristotle (340 BC), *Nicomachean Ethics,* ed. J. Henderson (1934), Loeb Classical Library 73, Cambridge Mass.: Harvard University Press

Ash, M.G. (2003), 'Psychology', in T.M. Porter & D. Ross (eds.), *The Cambridge History of Science: Vol. 7: The Modern Social Sciences*, Cambridge: Cambridge University Press, pp. 251–274

Atiyah, P.S. (1980), 'From Principles to Pragmatism', *Iowa Law Review*, **65**, pp. 1249–1272

Atiyah, P.S. & R.S. Summers (1987), *Form and Substance in Anglo-American Law*, Oxford: Oxford University Press

Backhouse, R.E. (1997), *Truth and Progress in Economic Knowledge*, Cheltenham: Edward Elgar

Bacon, F. (1620), *The New Organon,* ed. F.H. Anderson (1960), New York: The Liberal Arts Press

Baldwin, J. & G. Davis (2003), 'Empirical Research in Law', in P. Cane & M. Tushnet (eds.), *The Oxford Handbook of Legal Studies*, Oxford: Oxford University Press, pp. 880–900

Bar, C. Von & E. Clive (eds.) (2009a), *Principles, Definitions and Model Rules of European Private Law: Draft Common Frame of Reference*, München: Sellier

Bar, C. Von et al. (eds.) (2009b), *Principles, Definitions and*

Model Rules of European Private Law: Draft Common Frame of Reference: Outline edition, München: Sellier
Barendrecht, M. (2003), *Cooperation in transactions and disputes: a problem-solving legal system*, available at <www.ssrn.com> (accessed February 2012)
Becher, T. (1989), *Academic Tribes and Territories*, Milton Keynes: Open University Press
Beck, U. (2003), 'Toward a New Critical Theory with a Cosmopolitan Intent', *Constellations*, **10**, pp. 453–468
Becker, G.S. (1992), 'The Economic Way of Looking at Life', Nobel Lecture in Economics, available at <www.nobelprize.org> (accessed February 2012)
Bell, J. (2003), 'Legal Education', in P. Cane & M. Tushnet (eds.), *The Oxford Handbook of Legal Studies*, Oxford: Oxford University Press, pp. 901–919
Benda-Beckmann, F. Von (1979), *Property in Social Continuity*, The Hague: Nijhoff
Bentham, J. (1789), *An Introduction to the Principles of Morals and Legislation,* ed. J.H. Burns & H.L.A. Hart (1970), Oxford: Clarendon Press
Berlin, I. (1969), 'Two Concepts of Liberty', in *Four Essays on Liberty*, Oxford: Oxford University Press
Bernhart, C. (2008), *Regeln der Jurisprudenz: Die Grundsätze und Methoden der Rechtswissenschaft als Professionelle Standards*, Berlin: Duncker & Humblot
Bevan, G. & C. Hood (2006), 'What's Measured is What Matters: Targets and Gaming in the English Public Health Care System', *Public Administration*, **84**, pp. 517–538
Birks, P. (1985), *An Introduction to the Law of Restitution*, Oxford: Clarendon Press
Bix, B. (1996), *Jurisprudence: Theory and Context*, 5th ed., (2009), London: Sweet & Maxwell
Bok, D. (2004), *Universities in the Marketplace: The Commercialization of Higher Education*, Princeton: Princeton University Press
Bonnet, D. (2006), *L'Essentiel de la Méthodologie Juridique*, Paris: Ellipses

Boulton, G. and C. Lucas (2008), 'What are Universities for?', Position paper for League of European Research Universities, available at <www.leru.org> (accessed February 2012)

Bourdieu, P. (1984), *Distinction: A Social Critique of the Judgement of Taste*, translation by R. Nice of *La Distinction: Critique Sociale du Jugement* (1979), London: Routledge

Brown, R. (ed.) (2011), *Higher Education and the Market*, New York: Routledge

Bruijn, H. de (2002), *Managing Performance in the Public Sector*, London: Routledge

Burca, G. de (2008), 'Developing Democracy Beyond the State', *Columbia Journal of Transnational Law*, **46**, pp. 101–158

Bydlinski, F. (2003), *System und Prinzipien des Privatrechts*, Wien: Springer

Calliess, G.-P. & P. Zumbansen (2010), *Rough Consensus and Running Code: A Theory of Transnational Private Law*, Oxford: Hart Publishing

Canaris, C.-W. (1971), *Die Vertrauenshaftung im Deutschen Privatrecht*, München: Beck

Canaris, C.-W. (1983), *Systemdenken und Systembegriff in der Jurisprudenz*, Berlin: Duncker & Humblot

Chemerinsky, E. (2009), 'Why Write?' *Michigan Law Review*, **107**, pp. 881–894

Cicero (55 BC), *On the Orator*, ed. E.W. Sutton and H. Rackham (1942), Loeb CL 348, Cambridge Mass.: Harvard University Press

Coase, R.A. (1960), 'The Problem of Social Cost', *Journal of Law and Economics*, **3**, pp. 1–44

Collier, C.W. (1991), 'The Use and Abuse of Humanistic Theory in Law: Reexamining the Assumption of Interdisciplinary Legal Scholarship', *Duke Law Journal*, **41**, pp. 191–273

Cook, H. et al. (2009), 'Journals under Threat', *Medical History*, **53**, pp. 1–4

Cownie, F. (2004), *Legal Academics: Culture and Identities*, Oxford: Hart Publishing

Crombag, H.F.M. (2006), 'De Keuze van Hans Crombag', *De Academische Boekengids*, (issue 55), p. 19

Dannemann, G. (2006), 'Comparative Law: Study of Similarities or Differences?', in M. Reimann & R. Zimmermann (eds.), *The Oxford Handbook of Comparative Law*, Oxford: Oxford University Press, pp. 383–419

Darwin, C. (1859), *On The Origin of Species by Means of Natural Selection*, London: John Murray

Debreu, G. (1991), 'The Mathematization of Economic Theory', *American Economic Review*, **81**, pp. 1–7

Dennett, D.C. (1995), *Darwin's Dangerous Idea: Evolution and the Meanings of Life*, London: Allen Lane

Dilger, A. (2011), 'Die Gemeinschaft der Lehrenden und Lernenden', Centre for Interdisciplinary Economics Working Paper, University of Münster 1/2011, available at <www.wiwi.uni-muenster.de/ciw> (accessed February 2012)

Donohue, J. & J.J. Wolfers (2006), 'The Death Penalty: No Evidence for Deterrence', *The Economists' Voice*, (issue 3.5)

Dow, S.C. (2002), *Economic Methodology: An Inquiry*, Oxford: Oxford University Press

Dworkin, R. (1986), *Law's Empire*, Cambridge Mass.: Harvard University Press

Edmond, G. (2008), 'Judging the Scientific and Medical Literature: Some Legal Implications of Changes to Biomedical Research and Publication', *Oxford Journal of Legal Studies*, **28**, pp. 523–561

Edwards, H.T. (1992), 'The Growing Disjunction between Legal Education and the Legal Profession', *Michigan Law Review*, **91**, pp. 34–78

Ehrlich, E. (1913), *Fundamental Principles of the Sociology of Law*, translation by W.L. Moll (1936) of *Grundlegung der Soziologie des Rechts*, Cambridge Mass.: Harvard University Press

Ellickson, R.C. (1991), *Order Without Law: How Neighbors Settle Disputes*, Cambridge Mass.: Harvard University Press

Ellickson, R.C. (2000), 'Trends in Legal Scholarship: A Statistical Study', *Journal of Legal Studies*, **29**, pp. 517–543

Engel, C. & W. Schön (eds.) (2007), *Das Proprium der Rechtswissenschaft*, Tübingen: Mohr Siebeck

Engisch, K. (1956), *Einführung in das Juristische Denken*, 7th ed. (1977), Stuttgart: Kohlhammer

Epstein, L. & G. King (2002), 'The Rules of Inference', *University of Chicago Law Review*, **69**, pp. 1–133

Erasmus (1511), *In Praise of Folly*, translation by J. Wilson (2003) of *Stultitiae Laus*, Mineola: Dover Publications

European Commission (2010), *Assessing Europe's University-Based Research* (Report of the Expert Group), EUR 24187 EN, available at <http://ec.europa.eu/research-eu>

Faure, M.G. & J.M. Smits (eds.) (2011), *Does Law Matter? On Law and Economic Growth*, Cambridge-Antwerp: Intersentia

Feenstra, R. (1974), 'l'Influence de la Scolastique Espagnole sur Grotius en Droit Privé' (1973), in R. Feenstra, *Fata Iuris Romani*, Leyde: Presse Universitaire, pp. 338–363

Feinman, J.M. (1989), 'The Jurisprudence of Classification', *Stanford Law Review*, **41**, pp. 661–717

Feldbrugge, F.J.M. (ed.) (2003), *The Law's Beginnings*, Leiden: Nijhoff

Feyerabend, P.K. (1975), *Against Method*, London: Humanities Press

Feynman, R. (1964), *The Feynman Lectures on Physics*, Reading Mass.: Addison-Wesley

Feynman, R. (1999), *The Pleasure of Finding Things Out*, Cambridge Mass.: Perseus

Field, D.D. (1859), *The Magnitude and Importance of Legal Science*, New York: William J. Read

Finnis, J. (1980), *Natural Law and Natural Rights*, Oxford: Clarendon Press

Finnis, J. (1997), 'Commensuration and Public Reason', in R. Chang (ed.), *Incommensurability, Incomparability and Practical Reason*, Cambridge Mass.: Harvard University Press, pp. 215–233

Fish, S. (1984), 'Fish v. Fiss', *Stanford Law Review*, **36**, pp. 1325–1347
Fletcher, G.P. (1981), 'Two Modes of Legal Thought', *Yale Law Journal*, **90**, pp. 970–1003
Flyvbjerg, B. (2001), *Making Social Science Matter; Why Social Inquiry Fails and How It Can Succeed Again*, Cambridge: Cambridge University Press
Frey, B.S. & M. Osterloh (2006), *Evaluations: Hidden Costs, Questionable Benefits, and Superior Alternatives*, Institute for Empirical Research in Economics University of Zürich Working Paper 302, available at <www.ssrn.com> (accessed February 2012)
Fried, C. (1981), *Contract as Promise: A Theory of Contractual Obligation*, Cambridge Mass.: Harvard University Press
Friedman, D.D. (2000), *Law's Order: What Economics Has to Do with Law and Why It Matters*, Princeton: Princeton University Press
Friedman, L.M. (1973), *A History of American Law*, 3rd ed. (2005), New York: Simon and Schuster
Fuller, L. (1969), *The Morality of Law*, revised edition, New Haven: Yale University Press
Gadamer, H.-G. (1960), *Truth and Method*, translation by J. Weinsheimer & D.G. Marshall of *Wahrheit und Methode* (1981), London: Sheed and Ward
Gay, V. (2009), *Progress and Values in the Humanities: Comparing Culture and Science*, New York: Columbia University Press
Geertz, C. (2001), 'Empowering Aristotle: A Review', *Science*, **293** (5527), p. 53
Genn, H. (1999), *Paths to Justice*, Oxford: Hart Publishing
Gerven, W. van (1999), 'The Effect of Proportionality on the Actions of Member States of the European Community: National Viewpoints from Continental Europe', in E. Ellis (ed.), *The Principle of Proportionality in the Laws of Europe*, Oxford: Hart Publishing, pp. 37–63
Gestel, R. van & J. Vranken (2011), 'Assessing Legal Research: Sense and Nonsense of Peer Review versus Bibliometrics

and the Need for a European Approach', *German Law Journal*, **12**, pp. 901–929

Gestel, R. van & H.-W. Micklitz (2011), 'Revitalizing Doctrinal Legal Research in Europe: What about Methodology?', EUI Working Papers Law 2011/05, available at <www.ssrn.com> (accessed February 2012)

Glenn, H.P. (2003), 'A Transnational Concept of Law', in P. Cane & M. Tushnet (eds.), *The Oxford Handbook of Legal Studies*, Oxford: Oxford University Press, pp. 839–862

Glenn, H.P. (2006), 'Aims of Comparative Law', in J.M. Smits (ed.), *Elgar Encyclopedia of Comparative Law*, Cheltenham: Edward Elgar, pp. 57–65

Gordon, W.M. (2007), 'Legal Tradition, with Particular Reference to Roman Law', in W.M. Gordon, *Roman Law, Scots Law and Legal History: Selected Essays*, Edinburgh: Edinburgh University Press, pp. 362–375

Gould, S.J. (2003), *The Hedgehog, the Fox and the Magister's Pox*, New York: Harmony

Groot, A.D. de (1969), *Methodology: Foundations of Inference and Research in the Behavioural Sciences*, The Hague-Paris: Mouton

Grotius (1625), *De Jure Belli ac Pacis*, ed. De Kanter-van Hettinga Tromp/Feenstra (1993), Aalen: Scientia

Guerin, W. et al. (2010), *A Handbook of Critical Approaches to Literature*, 6th ed., Oxford: Oxford University Press

Habermas, J. (1968), *Knowledge and Human Interest*, translation by J. Knowlton & T. Cates (1987), of *Erkenntnis und Interesse*, Cambridge: Polity Press

Hage, J. (2011), 'The Method of a Truly Normative Legal Science', in M. Van Hoecke (ed.), *Methodologies of Legal Research*, Oxford: Hart Publishing, pp. 19–44

Hand, L. (1926), 'Have the Bench and the Bar Anything to Contribute to the Teaching of Law?', *Michigan Law Review*, **24**, pp. 466–482

Hart, H.L.A. (1961), *The Concept of Law*, 2nd ed. (1997), Oxford: Oxford University Press

Hayek, F.A. (1968), 'Competition as a Discovery Procedure', translation by M.S. Snow (2002), of 'Der Wettbewerb als Entdeckungsverfahren', *The Quarterly Journal of Austrian Economics*, **5**, pp. 9–23

Hayek, F.A. (1973–1979), *Law, Legislation and Liberty*, London: University of Chicago Press

Hayek, F.A. (1988), *The Fatal Conceit*, Chicago: University of Chicago Press

Heise, M. (2002), 'The Past, Present, and Future of Empirical Legal Scholarship: Judicial Decisionmaking and the New Empiricism', *University of Illinois Law Review*, pp. 819–850

Heringa, A.W. & Akkermans, B. (eds.) (2011), *Educating European Lawyers*, Cambridge, Antwerp: Intersentia

Hesen, G.G. (2009), 'The Empirics of Contracts', PhD thesis, Maastricht University

Hesselink, M.W. (2009), 'A European Legal Method? On European Private Law and Scientific Method', *European Law Journal*, **15**, pp. 20–45

Hesselink, M.W. (2010), 'A Spontaneous Order for Europe? Why Hayek's Libertarianism is Not the Right Way Forward for European Private Law', in H.W. Micklitz & F. Cafaggi (eds.), *After the Common Frame of Reference – What Future for European Private Law?*, Cheltenham: Edward Elgar, pp. 123–146

Heyne, P. et al. (1973), *The Economic Way of Thinking*, 10th ed. (2002), Upper Saddle River: Prentice Hall

Hobbes, T. (1681), *A Dialogue Between a Philosopher and A Student of the Common Laws of England*, ed. Q. Skinner (2005), Oxford: Clarendon Press

Hoebel, E.A. (1967), *The Law of Primitive Man,* (2006), Cambridge Mass.: Harvard University Press

Hoecke, M. Van (ed.) (2011), *Methodologies of Legal Research*, Oxford: Hart Publishing

Hoeren, T. (ed.) (2001), *Zivilrechtliche Entdecker*, München: Beck

Hoetink, H.R. (1929), 'On Understanding Foreign Law', translation by K. Maddock (1986) of 'Over Het Verstaan van Vreemd Recht', in *Opera Selecta*, Zutphen: Terra Publishing, pp. 23–52

Holleman, J.G. (ed.) (1981), *Van Vollenhoven on Indonesian Adat Law*, The Hague: Nijhoff

Holmes, O.W. (1870), 'Codes, and the Arrangement of the Law', *American Law Review* (1870), **5**, pp. 1–13

Holmes, O.W. (1881), *The Common Law*, ed. T.A. Schweich (2004), New York: Barnes & Noble

Holmes, O.W. (1897), 'The Path of the Law', *Harvard Law Review*, **10**, pp. 457–478

Horwitz, M. (1977), *The Transformation of American Law 1780–1860*, Cambridge Mass.: Harvard University Press

Hsieh, N. (2011), 'Incommensurable Values', in E.N. Zalta (ed.), *The Stanford Encyclopedia of Philosophy* (2011 Edition), available at <http://plato.stanford.edu/entries/value-incommensurable>

Huizinga, J. (1919), *The Waning of the Middle Ages*, translation by Fritz Hopman (1924) of *Herfsttij der Middeleeuwen*, London: Edward Arnold

Hume, D. (1748), *An Enquiry Concerning Human Understanding*, ed. L.A. Selby-Bigge (1975), 3rd ed., Oxford: Clarendon Press

Hunt, A. & G. Wickham (1994), *Foucault and Law: Towards a Sociology of Law as Governance*, London: Pluto

Husa, J. (2003), 'Farewell to Functionalism or Methodological Tolerance?' *Rabels Zeitschrift*, **67**, pp. 417–447

Husa, J. (2009), 'Turning the Curriculum Upside Down: Comparative Law as an Educational Tool for Constructing a Pluralistic Legal Mind', *German Law Journal*, **10**, pp. 913–928

Ibbetson, D. (2003), 'Historical Research in Law', in P. Cane & M. Tushnet (eds.), *Oxford Handbook of Legal Studies*, Oxford: Oxford University Press

Ijzermans, M.G. & G.A.F.M. van Schaaijk (1999), *Oefening Baart Kunst,* 3rd ed. (2007), Den Haag: Boom Juridische uitgevers

Ipsen, J. (2005), 'Ranking Juristischer Fakultäten in Deutschland', *Juristenzeitung* (2005), **60**, pp. 424–427

Jansen, N. (2005), 'Dogmatik, Erkenntnis und Theorie im Europäischen Privatrecht', *Zeitschrift für Europäisches Privatrecht*, **13**, pp. 750–783

Jansen, N. (2006), 'Comparative Law and Comparative Knowledge', in M. Reimann & R. Zimmermann (eds.), *The Oxford Handbook of Comparative Law*, Oxford: Oxford University Press, pp. 305–338

Jansen, N. & R. Michaels (2007), 'Private Law and the State', *Rabels Zeitschrift*, **71**, pp. 345–397

Jansen, N. (2010), *The Making of Legal Authority*, Oxford: Oxford University Press

Jestaz, Ph. & Ch. Jamin (2004), *La Doctrine*, Paris: Dalloz

Jhering, R. Von (1868), *Ist die Jurisprudenz eine Wissenschaft?* O. Behrends (ed.) (1998), Göttingen: Wallstein

Jhering, R. Von (1877), *Law as a Means to an End*, translation by Isaak Husik (1913) of *Der Zweck im Recht.* Boston: Boston Book Co.

John, E. & D. McIver Lopes (eds.) (2004), *The Philosophy of Literature*, Oxford: Blackwell

Jonsen, A.R. & S. Toulmin (1988), *The Abuse of Casuistry*, Berkeley: University of California Press

Kant, I. (1785), *Groundwork of the Metaphysics of Morals*, translation by M. Gregor (2002) of *Grundlegung zur Metaphysik der Sitten*, Cambridge: Cambridge University Press

Kantorowicz, H. (1906), 'The Battle for Legal Science,' translation by Cory Merrill (2011), of 'Der Kampf um die Rechtswissenschaft' *German Law Journal*, **12**, pp. 2005–2030

Kaplow, L. & S. Shavell (2002), *Fairness versus Welfare*, Cambridge Mass.: Harvard University Press

Kelsen, H. (1934), *Pure Theory of Law*, translation by Max Knight (1967) of *Reine Rechtslehre*, Los Angeles: University of California Press

Kennedy, D. (1976), 'Form and Substance in Private Law Adjudication', *Harvard Law Review*, **89**, pp. 1685–1778

Kirchmann, J. Von (1848), *Die Wertlosigkeit der Jurisprudenz als Wissenschaft*, Heidelberg: Manutius

Kleinwächter, F. (1883), *Die Kartelle: ein Beitrag zur Frage der Organisation der Volkswirtschaft*, Innsbrück: Wagner

KNAW (2005), *Judging Research on its Merits*, report by Council for the Humanities – Social Sciences Council, Amsterdam: Royal Netherlands Academy of Arts and Sciences

KNAW (2011), *Quality Indicators for Research in the Humanities*, Amsterdam: Royal Netherlands Academy of Arts and Sciences

Köndgen, J. (1981), *Selbstbindung ohne Vertrag*, Tübingen: Mohr Siebeck

Koopmans, T. (1991), 'Denken en Doen in het Recht' (1978), in T. Koopmans, *Juridisch Stippelwerk*, Deventer: Kluwer, pp. 67–75

Korobkin, R.B. (1999), 'Ranking Journals: Some Thoughts on Theory and Methodology', *Florida State University Law Review*, **26**, pp. 851–876

Korobkin, R.B. (2002), 'Empirical Scholarship in Contract Law: Possibilities and Pitfalls', *University of Illinois Law Review*, pp. 1033–1066

Kronman, A.T. (1980), 'Contract Law and Distributive Justice', *Yale Law Journal*, **89**, pp. 472–511

Kronman, A. (2007), *Education's End*, New Haven: Yale University Press

Kuhn, T. (1962), *The Structure of Scientific Revolution*, 2nd ed. (1970), Chicago: University of Chicago Press

Lagendijk, A. (1995), 'Voortdurend in Strijd met Concurrenten', *Atheneum Illustre*, **3** (September 1995), pp. 17–21

Lagendijk, A. (1997), 'Als het Moet sla ik Keihard Terug', interview *NRC Handelsblad*, 20 September 1997

Lagendijk, A. (1998), 'Bedrijfsongeluk', *De Volkskrant*, 11 April 1998

Larenz, K. (1960), *Methodenlehre der Rechtswissenschaft*, 6th ed. (1991), Berlin: Springer

Latour, B. (1987), *Science in Action: How to Follow Scientists and Engineers Through Society*, Cambridge Mass.: Harvard University Press

Lawson, T. (1996), 'The Predictive Science of Economics?', in S.G. Medema & W.J. Samuels (eds.), *Foundations of Research in Economics: How Do Economists Do Economics?*, Cheltenham: Edward Elgar, pp. 163–174

Leezenberg, M. & G. de Vries (2001), *Wetenschapsfilosofie voor geesteswetenschappen*, Amsterdam: Amsterdam University Press

Legrand, P. (1997), 'Against a European Civil Code', *Modern Law Review*, **60**, pp. 44–62

Leiter, B. (1996), 'Legal Realism', in D. Patterson (ed.), *A Companion to Philosophy of Law and Legal Theory*, Cambridge Mass.: Blackwell, pp. 261–279

Lessig, L. (2011), *Republic, Lost: How Money Corrupts Congress – and a Plan to Stop It*, New York: Twelve

Levitt, S.D. & J.J. Donohue (2001), 'The Impact of Legalized Abortion on Crime', *Quarterly Journal of Economics*, **116**, pp. 379–420

Levitt, S.D. & S.J. Dubner (2005), *Freakonomics*, New York: William Morrow

Lindo, C. (2009), 'Tussen Ideaal en Nuchterheid; Interview with the New President of the Hoge Raad, Mr G.J.M. Corstens', *Nederlands Juristenblad*, **84**, pp. 1074–1081

Lipstein, K. (1992), 'European Legal Education in the Future: Teaching the "Common Law of Europe"', in B. De Witte & C. Forder (eds.), *The Common Law of Europe and the Future of Legal Education*, Deventer: Kluwer, pp. 255–263

Llewellyn, K.N. (1930), *The Bramble Bush: On Our Law and Its Study*, New York: Oceana

Llewellyn, K.N. & E.A. Hoebel (1941), *The Cheyenne Way: Conflict and Case Law in Primitive Jurisprudence*, Norman: Oklahoma University Press

Lorenz, C. (ed.) (2008), *If You're So Smart, Why Aren't You Rich? Universiteit, Markt & Management*, Amsterdam: Boom

Low, G. (2010), *European Contract Law between the Single*

Market and the Law Market, PhD thesis, Maastricht University

Macaulay, S. (1963), 'Non-Contractual Relations in Business: a Preliminary Study', *American Sociological Review*, **28**, pp. 55–67

MacCormick, N. (1978), *Legal Reasoning and Legal Theory*, Oxford: Clarendon Press

MacIntyre, A.C. (1981), *After Virtue: A Study in Moral Theory*, Notre Dame: University of Notre Dame Press

Maine, H.J. Sumner (1861), *Ancient Law*, London: John Murray

Mak, C. (2007), 'Harmonising Effects of Fundamental Rights in European Contract Law', *Erasmus Law Review*, **1**, pp. 59–79

Markesinis, B.S. & J. Fedtke (2005), 'The Judge as Comparatist', *Tulane Law Review*, **80**, pp. 11–167

Martinek, M. (1991–1993), *Moderne Vertragstypen*, 3 vols., München: Beck

Mastronardi, P. (2001), *Juristisches Denken: Eine Einführung*, Stuttgart: UTB

Mataja, V. (1888), *Das Recht des Schadenersatzes vom Standpunkte der Nationalökonomie*, Leipzig: Duncker und Humblot

McCrudden, C. (2006), 'Legal Research and the Social Sciences', *Law Quarterly Review*, **122**, pp. 632–650

McKloskey, D.N. (1983), 'The Rhetoric of Economics', *Journal of Economic Literature*, **21**, pp. 481–517

Meijers, E.M. (1903), *Dogmatische Rechtswetenschap*, Amsterdam: Belinfante

Menand, L. (ed.) (1997), *Pragmatism*, New York: Vintage Books

Merton, R.K. & E. Barber (2006), *The Travels and Adventures of Serendipity*, Princeton: Princeton University Press

Merwe, D. van der (1996), 'Property in Mixed Legal Systems: South Africa', in G.E. van Maanen & A.J. van der Walt (eds.), *Property Law on the Threshold*, Antwerpen: Intersentia, pp. 355–389

Michaels, R. & N. Jansen (2006), 'Private Law Beyond the State? Europeanization, Globalization, Privatization', *American Journal of Comparative Law*, **54**, pp. 843–890

Michaels, R. (2011), 'Of Islands and the Ocean: the Two Rationalities of European Private Law', in R. Brownsword, H. Micklitz, L. Niglia & S. Weatherill (eds.), *The Foundations of European Private Law*, Oxford: Hart Publishing, pp. 139–158

Millgram, E. (1997), 'Incommensurability and Practical Reasoning', in R. Chang (ed.), *Incommensurability, Incomparability and Practical Reason*, Cambridge: Harvard University Press, pp. 151–169

Monateri, P.G. (2000), 'Black Gaius: A Quest for the Multicultural Origins of the "Western Legal Tradition"', *Hastings Law Journal*, **51**, pp. 479–555

Morgan, B. & K. Yeung (2007), *An Introduction to Law and Regulation*, Cambridge: Cambridge University Press

Morgan, M.S. (2003), 'Economics', in T.M. Porter & D. Ross (eds.), *The Cambridge History of Science Vol. 7: The Modern Social Sciences*, Cambridge: Cambridge University Press, pp. 275–305

Morisette, Y.-M. (2002), 'McGill's Integrated Civil and Common Law Program', *Journal of Legal Education*, **52**, pp. 12–28

Muir-Watt, H. (2011), 'The Epistemological Function of "la Doctrine"', in M. Van Hoecke, *Methodologies of Legal Research*, Oxford: Hart Publishing, pp. 123–131

Nuffield Foundation (2006), *Law in the Real World: Improving Our Understanding of How Law Works*, London, November 2006

Nussbaum, M.C. (1986), *The Fragility of Goodness*, Cambridge: Cambridge University Press

Nussbaum, M.C. (1995), *Poetic Justice: the Literary Imagination and Public Life*, Boston: Beacon Press

Nussbaum, M. (2003), 'Cultivating Humanity in Legal Education', *University of Chicago Law Review*, **70**, pp. 265–279

Ogus, A. (2006), *Costs and Cautionary Tales*, Oxford: Hart Publishing

Oostrom, F. van (2006), *Onderzoekend Onderwijs*, jaarrede KNAW, Amsterdam: KNAW

Oostrom, F. van (2007), *Markt en Ziel*, jaarrede KNAW, Amsterdam: KNAW

Osterloh, M. & B.S. Frey (2010), *Academic Rankings and Research Governance*, CREMA Working Paper 2010/2, available at <www.ssrn.com> (accessed February 2012), (revised German version published as *Die Krankheit der Wissenschaft* in *Frankfurter Allgemeine Zeitung* 21 July 2007, p. 13)

Patterson, D. (2001), 'Normativity and Objectivity in Law', *William & Mary Law Review*, **43**, pp. 325–363

Pels, D. (2003), *Unhastening Science; Autonomy and Reflexivity in the Social Theory of Knowledge*, Liverpool: Liverpool University Press

Perelman, C. (1980), *Justice, Law, and Argument: Essays on Moral and Legal Reasoning*, Dordrecht: Reidel

Pimont, S. (2006), 'A Propos de l'Activité Doctrinale Civiliste: Quelques Questions dans l'Air du Temps', *Revue Trimestrielle de Droit Civil*, pp. 707–718

Popper, K. (2002), *The Logic of Scientific Discovery* (1959), London: Routledge

Porter, T.M. (1995), *Trust in Numbers*, Princeton: Princeton University Press

Posner, E.A. (2000), *Law and Social Norms*, Cambridge Mass.: Harvard University Press

Posner, R.A. (1983), *The Economics of Justice*, Cambridge Mass.: Harvard University Press

Posner, R.A. (1987), 'The Decline of Law as an Autonomous Discipline 1962–1987', *Harvard Law Review*, **100**, pp. 761–780

Posner, R.A. (1990), *The Problems of Jurisprudence*, Cambridge Mass.: Harvard University Press

Posner, R.A. (1995), *Overcoming Law*, Cambridge Mass.: Harvard University Press

Posner, R.A. (2002), 'Legal Scholarship Today', *Harvard Law Review*, **115**, pp. 1314–1326

Posner, R.A. (2003), *Law, Pragmatism, and Democracy*, Cambridge Mass.: Harvard University Press

Posner, R.A. (2007), 'In Memoriam: Bernard D. Meltzer (1914–2007)', *University of Chicago Law Review*, **74**, pp. 435–438

Posner, R.A. (2011), *Economic Analysis of Law* (1972), 8th ed., New York: Aspen

Purnhagen, K. (2013), 'The Architecture of Post-National European Contract Law from a Phenomenological Perspective – A Question of Institutions', *Rabels Zeitschrift*, **77** (forthcoming)

Rakoff, T.D. & M. Minow (2007), 'A Case for Another Case Method', *Vanderbilt Law Review*, **60**, pp. 597–607

Rawls, J. (1971), *A Theory of Justice*, revised ed. (1999), Cambridge Mass.: Harvard University Press

Regini, M. (ed.) (2011), *European Universities and the Challenge of the Market*, Cheltenham: Edward Elgar

Rhode, D. (2002), 'Legal Scholarship', *Harvard Law Review*, **115**, pp. 1327–1361

Riley, K.F. & M.P. Hobson (2006), *Mathematical Methods for Physics and Engineering*, Cambridge: Cambridge University Press

Rosenberg, A. (1992), *Economics – Mathematical Politics or Science of Diminishing Returns*, Chicago: University of Chicago Press

Rothacker, E. (1954), *Die Dogmatische Denkform in den Geisteswissenschaften und das Problem des Historismus*, Akad. der Wissenschaften und der Literatur; Abh. der Geistes und Soz.w. Kl. 1954–6, Mainz: Akademie der Wissenschaften und der Literatur

Ruane, J.M. (2005), *Essentials of Research Methods: A Guide to Social Science Research*, Oxford: Blackwell

Rubin, E.L. (1988), 'The Practice and Discourse of Legal Scholarship', *Michigan Law Review*, **86**, 1835–1905

Rubin, E.L. (1996), 'Legal Scholarship', in D. Patterson

(ed.), *A Companion to Philosophy of Law and Legal Theory*, Cambridge Mass.: Blackwell, pp. 562–572

Saffer, H. & F. Chaloupka (2000), 'The Effect of Tobacco Advertising Bans on Tobacco Consumption', *Journal of Health Economics*, **19**, pp. 1117–1137

Salmon, M.H. et al. (eds.) (1999), *Introduction to the Philosophy of Science*, Indianapolis: Hackett

Samuel, G. (2008), 'Is Law Really a Social Science? A View from Comparative Law', *Cambridge Law Journal*, **67**, pp. 288–321

Samuel, G. (2009), 'Can Legal Reasoning be Demystified?', *Legal Studies*, **29**, pp. 181–210

Sandel, M.J. (2009), *Justice: What's The Right Thing To Do?* London: Allen Lane

Savigny, F.C. Von (1814), *Of the Vocation of our Age for Legislation and Jurisprudence*, translation by Abraham Hayward (1831) of *Vom Beruf unsrer Zeit für Gesetzgebung und Rechtswissenschaft*, London: Littlewood

Savigny, F.C. Von (1840–1848), *System of the Modern Roman Law*, translation by William Holloway (1979) of *System des Heutigen Römischen Recht*, Westport Conn.: Hyperion Press

Scalia, A. (1996), 'Commentary', *St. Louis University Law Journal*, **40**, pp. 1119–1122

Schama, S. (1987), *The Embarrassment of Riches*, London: Collins

Schauer, F. (2009), *Thinking Like a Lawyer*, Cambridge Mass.: Harvard University Press

Schneider, L. et al. (1981), 'Government Regulation of Cigarette Health Information', *Journal of Law & Economics*, **24**, pp. 575–612

Schoordijk, H.C.F. (1972), *Oordelen en Vooroordelen*, Deventer: Kluwer

Schröder, J. (2001), *Recht als Wissenschaft*, München: Beck

Schroeder, J.L. (2002), *Apples and Oranges: The Commensurability Debate in Legal Scholarship*, Cardozo

Law School Public Law Paper 48, available at <www.ssrn.com> (accessed February 2012)

Schweber, H. (1999), 'The "Science" of Legal Science: The Model of the Natural Sciences in Nineteenth-Century American Legal Education', *Law and History Review*, **17**, pp. 421–466

Shapin, S. (2008), *The Scientific Life: A Moral History of a Late Modern Vocation*, Chicago: University of Chicago Press

Shaughnessy, J. et al. (1985), *Research Methods in Psychology*, 9th ed., (2011), Boston: McGraw Hill

Shleifer, A. & E.L. Glaeser (2002), 'Legal Origins', *Quarterly Journal of Economics*, **117**, pp. 1193–1229

Siems, M.M. (2008), 'Legal Originality', *Oxford Journal of Legal Studies*, **28**, pp. 147–162

Singer, J.W. (2009), 'Normative Methods for Lawyers', *UCLA Law Review*, **56**, pp. 899–982

Smith, H. (2009), *Individual and Institutional Authority: The Turn-of-the-Century Quest to Abolish the Dissenting Opinion*, Yale Law School Student Prize Papers, available at <www.ssrn.com> (accessed February 2012)

Smith, S.D. (1992), 'In Defense of Traditional Legal Scholarship: A Comment', *University of Colorado Law Review*, **63**, pp. 627–640

Smits, J.M. (2002a), *The Making of European Private Law*, Antwerp, Oxford, New York: Intersentia

Smits, J.M. (2002b), 'How to Predict the Differences in Uniformity between Different Areas of a Future European Private Law? An Evolutionary Approach', in A. Marciano & J.-M. Josselin (eds.), *The Economics of Harmonizing European Law*, Cheltenham: Edward Elgar, pp. 50–70

Smits, J.M. (ed.) (2005), *The Need for a European Contract Law*, Groningen: Europa Law Publishing

Smits, J.M. (2006), 'Comparative Law and its Influence on National Legal Systems', in M. Reimann & R. Zimmermann (eds.), *The Oxford Handbook of Comparative Law*, Oxford: Oxford University Press, pp. 477–512

Smits, J.M. (2008a), 'Human Dignity and Uniform Law: an Unhappy Relationship', in Olivier Moréteau, Julio Romanach, Alberto Zuppi (eds.), *Essays in Honor of Saúl Litvinoff*, Baton Rouge: Claitor, pp. 749–760

Smits, J.M. (2008b), 'The German Schuldrechtsmodernisierung and the New Dutch Civil Code: a Study in Parallel', in O. Remien (ed.), *Schuldrechtsmodernisierung und Europäisches Vertragsrecht*, Tübingen: Mohr Siebeck, pp. 117–131

Smits, J.M. (2009a), 'Democracy and European Private Law', *European Journal of Legal Studies*, **2**, pp. 26–40

Smits, J.M. (2009b), 'Redefining Normative Legal Science: Towards an Argumentative Discipline', in F. Coomans et al. (eds.), *Methods of Human Rights Research*, Antwerp, Oxford: Intersentia, pp. 45–58

Smits, J.M. (2010), 'The Draft Common Frame of Reference: How to Improve it?', in H.W. Micklitz & F. Cafaggi (eds.), *European Private Law after the Common Frame of Reference – What Future for European Private Law?*, Cheltenham: Edward Elgar, pp. 99–100

Smits, J.M. (2011), 'European Legal Education, or: How to Prepare Students for Global Citizenship?', *The Law Teacher*, **45**, pp. 163–180

Snow, C.P. (1959), *The Two Cultures*, ed. S. Collini (1993), Cambridge: Cambridge University Press

Sokal, A.D. (1996), 'A Physicist Experiments with Cultural Studies', *Lingua Franca* May/June 1996, pp. 62–64

Stein, E. (2000), *Die Rechtswissenschaftliche Arbeit*, Tübingen: Mohr Siebeck

Stigler, G. (1963), *The Intellectual and the Marketplace and Other Essays*, London: Free Press

Stigler, G.J. (1965), The Economist and the State, *American Economic Review*, **55**, pp. 1–18

Stolker, C.J.J.M. (2003), '"Ja, Geléérd zijn Jullie Wel!": over de Status van de Rechtswetenschap', *Nederlands Juristenblad*, **78**, pp. 766–778

Stolker, C.J.J.M. (2005), 'Legal Journals: In Pursuit of a More

Scientific Approach', *European Journal of Legal Education*, **2**, pp. 77–94

Strauss, P. (2006), 'Transsystemia: Are We Approaching a New Langdellian Moment?' *Journal of Legal Education*, **56**, pp. 161–171

Strijbosch, F. (1996), 'De Rechtsantropologie in Nederland en in België', in J. Griffiths (ed.), *De Sociale Werking van Recht*, 3rd ed., Nijmegen: Ars Aequi, pp. 534–542

Study Group on Social Justice in European Private Law (2004), 'Social Justice in European Contract Law: a Manifesto', *European Law Journal*, **10**, pp. 653–674

Sunstein, C.R. & A. Vermeule (2006), 'Is Capital Punishment Morally Required? Acts, Omissions, and Life-Life Tradeoffs', *Stanford Law Review*, **58**, pp. 703–750

Sunstein, C.R. & J. Wolfers (2008), 'A Death Penalty Puzzle: The Murky Evidence For and Against Deterrence', *The Washington Post,* 30 June 2008, p. A11

Supiot, A. (2005), *Homo Juridicus: Essai sur la Fonction Anthropologique du Droit*, Paris: Seuil

Tallon, D. (1998), 'Les Faux Amis en Droit Comparé', in J. Basedow et al. (eds.), *Festschrift für Ulrich Drobnig zum siebztigen Geburtstag*, Tübingen: Mohr Siebeck, pp. 677–682

Tamanaha, B.Z. (2006), *Law as a Means to an End: Threat to the Rule of Law*, Cambridge: Cambridge University Press

Tao, T. (2007), 'What is Good Mathematics?', *Bulletin of the American Mathematical Society*, **44**, pp. 623–634, available at <http://arXiv:math/0702396v1>

Tettinger, P.J. & T. Mann (2009), *Einführung in die Juristische Arbeitstechnik*, 4th ed., München: Beck

Teubner, G. (1997), 'Breaking Frames: The Global Interplay of Legal and Social Systems', *American Journal of Comparative Law*, **45**, pp. 149–169

Thiel, S. van & F.L. Leeuw (2002), 'The performance paradox in the public sector', *Public Performance & Management Review*, **25**, pp. 267–281

Tijssen, H.E.B. (2009), 'De Juridische Dissertatie Onder de Loep', PhD thesis, Tilburg University

Tiller, E.H. & F.B. Cross (2006), 'What is Legal Doctrine?' *Northwestern University Law Review*, **100**, pp. 517–534
Toulmin, S. (1990), *Cosmopolis: The Hidden Agenda of Modernity*, New York: Free Press
Twining, W. (1994), *Blackstone's Tower: The English Law School*, London: Stevens & Sons
Twining, W. & D.R. Miers (1976), *How To Do Things With Rules,* 5th ed. (2010), Cambridge: Cambridge University Press
Ulen, T.S. (2002), A Nobel Prize in Legal Science: Theory, Empirical Work, and the Scientific Method in the Study of Law, *University of Illinois Law Review*, pp. 875–920
Unger, R.M. (1986), *The Critical Legal Studies Movement*, Cambridge Mass.: Harvard University Press
Vogenauer, S. (2006), 'An Empire of Light? II: Learning and Lawmaking in Germany Today', *Oxford Journal of Legal Studies*, **26**, pp. 627–663
Vranken, J.B.M. (2006), *Exploring the Jurist's Frame of Mind*, Deventer: Kluwer
VSNU (2005), Report *Oordelen over Rechten* (Stolker report), Commissie Voorbereiding Onderzoeksbeoordeling Rechtsgeleerdheid, Den Haag: Association of Universities in the Netherlands
VSNU (2007), Report *Naar Prestatie-Indicatoren voor Rechtswetenschappelijk Onderzoek* (Smits report), Commissie Prestatie-indicatoren en Ranking, Den Haag: Association of Universities in the Netherlands
Walt, A.J. van der (1995), 'Marginal notes on Powerful Legends: Critical Perspectives on Property Theory', *Tydskrif vir Hedendaagse Romeins-Hollandse Reg*, **58**, pp. 396–420
Watson, A. (1994), 'The Importance of "Nutshells"', *American Journal of Comparative Law*, **42**, pp. 1–23
Watson, A. (2006), *The Shame of American Legal Education*, Lake Mary: Vandeplas Publishing
Weber, M. (1922), *Economy and Society*, translation by E. Fischoff (1968), of *Wirtschaft und Gesellschaft*, New York: Bedminster Press

Weber, M. (1922), 'Science as a Vocation', translation by H.H. Gerth & C. Wright Mills of 'Wissenschaft als Beruf' in H.H. Gerth & C. Wright Mills (ed.) (1946), *From Max Weber: Essays in Sociology*, New York: Oxford University Press, pp. 129–156

Weinrib, E.J. (1995), *The Idea of Private Law*, Cambridge Mass.: Harvard University Press

Wendt, J.A.I. (2008), *De Methode der Rechtswetenschap Vanuit Kritisch-Rationeel Perspectief,* PhD thesis, Erasmus University Rotterdam

Wilburg, W. (2000), *The Development of a Flexible System in the Area of Private Law*, translation by Herbert Hausmaninger of *Entwicklung eines Beweglichen Systems im Bürgerlichen Recht* (1950), Wien: Manzsche Verlag

Wilhelmsson, T. (2002), 'The Legal, the Cultural and the Political: Conclusions from Different Perspectives on Harmonisation of European Contract Law', *European Business Law Review*, **13**, pp. 541–556

Wilson, E.O. (1998), *Consilience: The Unity of Knowledge*, London: Little, Brown and Company

Wright, G.H. Von (1971), *Explanation and Understanding*, London: Routledge & Kegan Paul

Zelst, B. van (2008), *The Politics of European Sales Law*, The Hague: Kluwer Law International

Zimmermann, R. (1990), *The Law of Obligations: Roman Foundations of the Civilian Tradition*, Cape Town: Juta

Zimmermann, R. (1997), 'The Civil Law in European Codes', in D.L. Carey Miller & R. Zimmermann (eds.), *The Civilian Tradition and Scots Law*, Berlin: Duncker & Humblot, pp. 259–293

Zumbansen, P. & G.-P. Calliess (eds.) (2011), *Law, Economics and Evolutionary Theory*, Cheltenham: Edward Elgar

Zweigert, K. (1964), 'Seriozitätsindizien', *Juristenzeitung*, **19**, pp. 349–353

Index

The numbers refer to the sections.